To all the children of the world who don't have access to clean water and healthy environments.

Produced by SilverPen Studios.
Illustrators: Jessica Pierce and Christina Spinks
Design and formatting: Sarah Donnelly

**Table of Contents**

Hey, we're the Science Kids! Thanks for joining us on this journey to explore one of the most amazing things in the universe: YOUR BRAIN!!!

In this book, we will learn about 7 important things: Understanding the Science, Mind Power, Eating Healthy, Exercise, Sleep, Relaxation, and Planning. In abbreviation: UMEESRP! Hmm, UMEESRP doesn't cut it. Let's do our first mind exercise: how many ways can you reorder UMEESRP so it sounds cool? Hint: it's the title of the book!

That's right: SUPER ME!

# Science Key

 **Did You Know?**          Learn something you didn't know.

 **Fun Fact!**          Learn a new fun fact about science!

 **Amazing Animals!**          Animals and science are amazing!

 **Tip!**          A new tool to incorporate.

 **Bonus!**          Learn more!

 **Hint!**          Heres a hint to help you out!

 **Rule of Tumb!**          A good rule to follow if you are not sure!

 **Weird and Wacky**          Weird fun facts that are so interesting!

# Getting Started

As a human being, you are incredibly complex. Muscles, nerves, organs, and the rest of your body all work together, but of all the organs, the most important is your brain.

Your brain is sort of like a really powerful and squishy computer that helps you do everything you do. Since your brain works so hard and never takes any time off (even when you sleep), you need to treat it well! And as you take care of your brain, you take care of the rest of your body at the same time. You can do that by eating well, sleeping the right amount, and doing a few other things we'll talk about in this book.

# Chapter 1
# Understanding the Science

As young scientists, we know it's important to ask questions. They say there's no such thing as a dumb question, and when it comes to science, this is true! You gotta ask questions to learn! Once you ask a question, as a scientist, you can investigate and observe to find the answers. Observations might be made with tools or with your own senses.

You can collect data, write down your observations, and come up with a conclusion. Experiments can show whether that conclusion is correct. The neat thing about science is once you come to that conclusion then other scientists can repeat your experiment to see if they agree. If other scientists agree, then it's probable that you are correct!

We Agree!

The scientific method starts with asking questions. These questions could include What, Why, How, When, Who, Which, or Where? For example:

- What is memory?
- Why do we remember some things and forget others?
- How can we improve our memory?
- Where are memories stored?
- Which tools can we use to improve memory?

To answer those questions, scientists start with a hypothesis. A hypothesis is basically just an educated guess about the answer. It often includes a prediction about what will happen. "If (I do this), then (this will happen)."

Of course, for a hypothesis to be useful to you and to others, you need to test it. For instance, you could hypothesize "If I flap my arms fast, then I will fly".

But once you test that hypothesis, you will learn that's a false one. No matter how fast you flap, you won't fly. So for a hypothesis to be useful, it needs to be something you can prove and repeat, like: "If I flap my arms fast enough, I can move a pin wheel."

If not, you can change your hypothesis and design new experiments based on the new hypothesis. Like, in the pinwheel example, you might need to use a different pinwheel or wave your hands harder. If the experiment shows the hypothesis to be true, more work needs to be done. You may want to figure out the slowest you can wave your arms and still power the pinwheel. Or you may want to see if you can spin the pinwheel with burps. Science has no boundaries!

The experiment may be repeated many times in order to make sure the results are always the same. Other scientists should also be able to repeat the experiment and get the same result. If many experiments show the same answers, we can be pretty sure the answers are right. Science likes to verify. Science is not an opinion about what you think will work or how you want something to work.

## The Scientific Method

Science: The knowledge or study of the natural world based on facts. These facts are learned through experiments and observation. For instance, if you let go of a ball, it will fall down, thanks to gravity.

Scientific method: A way of doing research. A problem is identified and data (pieces of information) are gathered. Then the scientist forms a hypothesis (an educated guess). Finally, the hypothesis is tested through controlled experiments (tests).

To be scientific, the method needs to study evidence that can be measured. It also needs to stand to scientific reasoning (scientific reasoning uses logic based on what you already know).

In other words, scientists ask questions and use evidence to answer them. The answers cannot simply be guesses or 'what makes sense'. Scientists look for proof. Often, science means admitting, "Oops, I was wrong. Back to the drawing board!"

However, science is a process that can take many years. The human body is very complex, with many systems that work together. That means understanding human health can be tricky.

Still, scientists have been working hard for centuries to understand what makes us healthy. They may not have all the answers, but they have good methods that have allowed us to discover and do amazing things, such as discovering vaccines that have saved lives from devastating infections that killed millions of people!

# Chapter 2
# Mind Powers

## True or False

1. We only use 10 percent of our brains.

2. We are either "left brain" logical people or "right brain" creative people.

3. Female and male brains are different, so girls and boys learn differently.

4. We each have a different learning style. Some people learn stuff better by seeing it, and some learn stuff better by hearing it.

5. People can sometimes recover from brain damage.

6. A blind person may be able to hear better than the average person.

7. Can your brain really fart? Okay, we'll answer that one now: nope, it can't! We're just testing to make sure you're paying attention!

Find the answers at the end of the chapter, except for the brain fart question, of course.

## Your amazing brain

Your brain only weighs about two to three pounds. In other words, your brain is about the size of a very fat hamster, yet your brain is incredibly complex! The brain is made up of several specialized cells that all work together all the time. The brain is always doing something! You think with your brain, of course. Thinking includes making judgments and solving problems. One part of your brain processes what you hear and another part processes what you see.

Your brain is also responsible for voluntary movements. That's when you decide to move, like scratching your head, dancing on one leg, or kicking a soccer ball. It is responsible for your balance and coordination, too. It keeps you from falling over after kicking that soccer ball. Your brain also controls your body's basic functions, such as breathing. Finally, if you remember any of this later, which we hope you do, then you can thank your brain for that. Brains are way cool!

Kicking a soccer ball uses many parts of your brain.

You see the ball coming (visual processing)

You hear shouts from your teammates (auditory processing)

You decide to kick the ball (making a judgment)

You figure out how you need to move (solving a problem)

You shift your weight to one foot (using balance)

You swing your leg (muscles control)

Meanwhile, you continue breathing (maintaining basic functions) - it would be annoying if you had to think "breath" every few seconds!

You mentally record this experience so you can talk about it later over ice cream with your buddies. Hopefully you'll be saying, "Man, that was an awesome goal!"

This page is about me!

## The Brain Throughout History

Early people did not know that the brain was the center of intelligence. The ancient Egyptians and Greeks believed the heart was the center of intelligence. Maybe that's where the saying, "find it in your heart" comes from?

In the second century A.D., the Roman physician named Galen, stated that the brain is the center of intelligence and not the heart! Yet for centuries people disagreed with him!

Artist and inventor Leonardo da Vinci was one of the first to make accurate diagrams of the brain by the early 16th century. Leonardo may have been one of the smartest people in history!

In the 16th and 17th centuries, anatomy experts named many parts of the brain. Yet they had little understanding of how those parts worked. Actually, we're STILL trying to understand the brain better!

# Parts of the brain

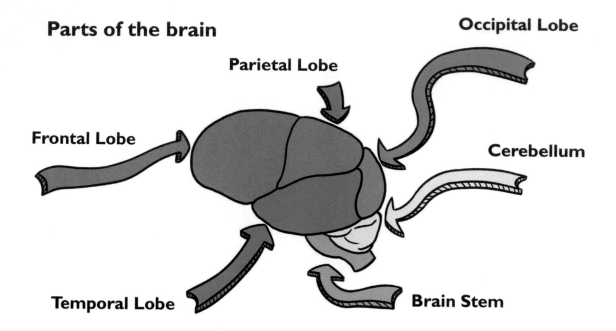

**Occipital Lobe**

**Parietal Lobe**

**Frontal Lobe**

**Cerebellum**

**Temporal Lobe**

**Brain Stem**

## Brain Vocabulary!

**Cerebrum:** Performs all complex functions. Your cerebrum is firing away right now as you read these words.

**Parietal Lobe:** Helps you interpret sensation, understand numbers, objects, shapes and space. For instance, it helps you turn the pages of this book.

**Occipital Lobe:** Responsible for processing what you see. The occipital lobe allows you to see these words right now.

**Cerebellum:** Controls movement and balance. It's helping you move your eyes smoothly right now!

**Frontal Lobe:** Helps you predict the consequences of actions and choose between good and bad actions. This helps you make "executive decisions" like, 'Should I watch YouTube or do my homework?'

**Temporal Lobe:** Helps you interpret what you hear, and recognize and remember things you see, like these words you're reading now.

**Brainstem:** Transfers information between the brain and other parts of the body and controls involuntary functions, such as breathing.

You can see that multiple parts of the brain are always working together to help you make sense of the world around you!

So why is the human brain special? It's definitely not because of its size. Other animals have bigger brains than ours. Even our ancient ancestors, the Neanderthals, had bigger brains than we do. So when it comes to brains, bigger isn't always better. What does matter are brain cell, how these are connected, and how we use those connections.

## Fun Fact!

Did you know that some people have to have one hemisphere of the brain removed? The other half takes over the responsibilities of the removed half.

Neurons are special nerve cells. They carry messages between the brain and other parts of the body. Your brain may have over 80 billion neurons! You don't have to be a math whiz to know that's A LOT!

Information from one neuron flows to another neuron across a synapse. Each neuron in the human brain can form tens of thousands of synapses! Think of it as a big tree with thousands of branches zapping information to other trees through their branches using electricity! Wow! That's a lot of information zipping around!

The human brain is different from other animal brains because it does so much more than just help us move, sense and feel. The human cerebral cortex, the outer layer of the brain, helps us organize, reason, read, write, play music and solve problems. Whenever you think about anything, 'Why am I here?', 'What should I have for lunch?' or 'Blue is a really cool color!', that's the cerebral cortex at work.

**Fun Fact!**

The human brain weighs about 3 pounds. An elephant's brain weighs about 9 pounds. A whale's brain can weigh up to 17 pounds! In general, the bigger the animal, the bigger its brain. tThe size of a brain does not determine intelligence. A mouse's brain is smaller than a penny, yet a mouse can make decisions, learn, work mazes, and communicate with other mice. Dinosaurs had HUGE brains but none of them could ever work their way through a maze!

## How much do our brains change?

Your brain starts growing before you are born. It develops greatly during childhood, but the changes aren't just growth. In the first year of life, a baby's brain grows intensely. Synapses, or the connections between neurons, develop all over the place. But after that, the brain actually starts losing some cells. It keeps important ones like those that help the child perceive and understand the world. The brain prunes out the unnecessary cells, like a gardener pulling weeds so the flowers can grow better.

This combination of growth and pruning continues throughout childhood till you become an adult. How you use your brain will determine what parts grow and what parts are pruned. In childhood, you can learn all kinds of things more easily than adults can. Your young brain is more flexible and can adapt better to change. So if you want to learn something complicated like computer programming, do it now!

There are a lot of advantages to having a young, growing brain. However, there are risks as well. Since your brain is growing, it's more vulnerable to damage. For example, in kids and teens, alcohol and tobacco can damage parts of the brain involved in memory. These effects last much longer than childhood or teenagehood. Heavy alcohol use isn't healthy for any brain, but it's worse for children and teenagers. That is why it is very important to avoid these things.

## Protecting your brain

You can do many things to keep your brain healthy. One of the most important things you can do is protect your brain from injury. After all, you only get one brain and it has to last you a long time. You know how people used to say "YOLO!"? Well, now there's "YOHOB", which means, you only have one brain!

Thousands of children and teenagers are treated for head injuries every year. Often, these injuries are caused by sports and similar activities. Fights, falls, and car accidents can also cause brain injuries.

Your brain is soft and squishy! You skull forms a protective hard cover around it, and fluid keeps the brain cushioned inside your skull, but sometimes that's not enough. You know how when the car stops fast, you keep moving? That is exactly like the brain. When your head hits something or stops suddenly, the brain keeps moving and can hit the skull. It's kind of like bruising your brain. A blow or bump of the head that causes damage is called a concussion. Concussions must be treated properly. If you hit your head, tell an adult or a doctor right away.

If you get injured while playing sports, sit out the rest of the game. Especially if you see "stars". Stars may look cool, but this is a sign that you really need to sit and rest, and probably get checked out!

If you can't remember what day it is or don't know where you are or what your name is, see a doctor!

**Amazing Animals!**

- The silk worm has 11 brains but only uses five of them. Guess it doesn't hurt to have a few spares!

- Starfish do not have brains.

- The honeybee may be the smartest insect. After all, spelling bees are named after them.

- The sperm whale has the biggest brain, weighing up to 20 pounds. Wow! Hope it's not letting its big head get to it!

- The giant squid's brain is shaped like a doughnut. The brain circles around the squid's esophagus, so every meal passes through the brain. Talk about wrapping your mind around it!

- The bird called the Clark's Nutcracker buries about 30,000 pine nuts a year. It remembers where at least 70% of them are. You might say these birds go nuts!

## Can memory improve?

Memory can vary greatly from one person to another. Memory seems to depend on several factors. Genetics - what you are given at birth - is a part of it. But training can seriously improve your memory. People with great memories have usually improved through practice. In fact, some memory champions (yes, they do have memory contests) have taught themselves to super charge their memories. It is also possible to have a good memory in some areas and not in others. For example, an expert chess player may be able to play blindfolded, remembering where all the pieces are on the board, but they may not have an amazing memory about other things.

Experts say we are all capable of having a better memory. Part of the problem is remembering to remember. If you meet someone new, but can't remember their name later, you probably never really learned the name in the first place. Maybe you were paying more attention to the person's clothes or something else. Maybe you were wondering what to have for dinner. With all that other information coming in, your brain didn't bother to remember the name. Brains are amazing but even they have limits!

**Tip!**

Don't leave the T.V. on when you study. Eliminate distractions and avoid doing several things at once (multitasking). Research shows that multitasking makes it hard to lock memories in your brain!

## Set up a reminder

If you have a computer or cell phone, you may be able to set up a reminder on a digital calendar. Then, it will set off an alarm or send you a message. You can also use a paper calendar, make a to-do list, or leave yourself notes. It may take a while to get used to using them at first. You'll have to remember to check the calendar or look at the list, but over time you'll build new habits. Like everything else, the more you do it, the better you'll get at it!

## Repeat yourself

When you learn something new, it enters your short-term memory. But, short-term memories may only last a minute or two. That's why they're called short-term, though a better name might be short-lasting. If you want to remember the information, you need to move it to your long-term memory. One way to make it long-term is to repeat the information. When you meet someone new, say their name out loud. If possible, use their name two or three times while you're talking to them.

Repeating information out loud can also help if you tend to forget what you were trying to do.

Let's say your mom asks you to take out the kitchen garbage. As you walk towards the kitchen, you think about other things. By the time you get to the kitchen, you've forgotten why you went there. You ignore the garbage and get a snack, and then you get in trouble. You can avoid this by repeating, "I'm going to take out the garbage," as you walk to the kitchen. You might want to turn it into a song or make a rhyme out of it: Oh wow and holy cow, we're takin' out the garbage now!

Let's say you often forget to take your lunch to school. Make a list of the things you need to do before leaving the house. Every morning, repeat that list out loud as you do those things in the same order. "I'm brushing my teeth, I'm putting my homework in my bag, I'm getting my lunch..." This will help lock the routine in your mind!

## Did You Know?

Studies have found that walking through a doorway makes you forget. It's as if your brain decides that you went through a giant eraser, so you can forget what happened in the last room. As you go into the new room, say out loud what you were planning to do. This will help reverse the 'doorway effect', or as we like to call it, the 'giant eraser effect'.

"♪" Radio Jingle,
♪ Commercial Song!
Stuck in your head,
So very long! ♪

## Use sounds and meanings

Remember how the brain has different parts, and some parts are related to different senses, such as sound or smell? Using several senses might help you lock information into different parts of your brain. For example, say you want to remember the parts of the brain. Make your own drawing and label the parts, saying the parts out loud. Doing something yourself will usually help you remember more than just looking at someone else's drawing. Act out a scene from history to help you remember what happened, or draw a comic strip of the event. Color can also help you remember! Use colored pens to highlight important ideas when you study. Or even doodle your important notes. And most importantly, add emotions!

Music is another big boost to memory. First of all, you can listen to music to adjust your energy level. If you're tired and unmotivated, play some bouncy music to get your energy level up. If you're anxious and can't focus, play something calm to help you relax. You've heard the phrase, 'You are what you eat', but your mindset can also be influenced by what you listen to as well! Mood music really can change your mood! (See the chapter on Relaxation for more tips on getting in the right frame of mind.)

As we mentioned a bit earlier, you can even make up a song about information you want to remember. Studies have shown that it's easier to remember a rhyme than something that isn't rhymed. This is why we learn, "In 1492, Columbus sailed the ocean blue." The rhyme of 'blue' and 'two' make it easier to recall the date.

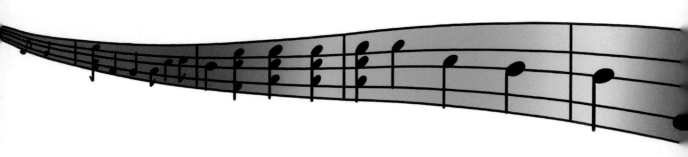

Other studies show that people remember words better when they sing them instead of merely speaking them. Even saying words in a singsong voice works, especially for lists of items. For generations, children have learned the alphabet by singing the "ABC" song. The song is simply reciting the alphabet, but with a tune that helps you remember it.

Making up a rhyme may also help you recall important main ideas. People who make commercials know this. That's why they make little musical jingles about their products: people hear the jingle a few times on T.V. or the radio, and when they see the product in the store, the song starts playing in their head and they're more likely to buy.

You can use the same trick to remember important information, whether it's your address and phone number for emergencies, or study material for a test. Rhyme it and sing it! Bet you never would have thought that learning could be so musical!

Explain what you've learned to someone else, even a pet or stuffed animal. Explaining the information aloud, in your own words, can help you remember it. Plus your pet might learn something!

## Did You Know?

There is no such thing as true photographic memory. Most of us can remember the things we've seen fairly well. For example, for most people, it's easier to recognize someone's face than their name. After all, humans have been remembering faces for a lot longer than humans have had names! Some people may be especially good at remembering things they see, but there is no proof that anyone can actually remember what they've seen in photographic detail.

The closest thing to photographic memory is eidetic memory. Someone who has this ability can 'see' an image after it's been removed. For example, they might look at a photo for 30 seconds. Once the photo is removed, they still 'see' it, and they can describe its details. However, they may not describe everything accurately, and their accuracy quickly gets worse. After a few minutes, they may not remember any more than the average person.

Since humans are especially good at remembering places like their homes and streets, one technique memory champs use is called 'Memory Palaces'. Very simply, memory palaces are where they relate an object to memorize to a room in a place that they know well. Memory champs using this technique have been able to memorize card sequences of over 2000 cards!

Fun Note:
Yu cn mst lkly rd ths! Th brn flls n th blnks!

## Group things together

It's easier to remember 15, 27, and 92 than it is to remember 1, 5, 2, 7, 9, and 2. This technique of organizing information into small groups is sometimes called "chunking". You can do this with any type of information, and it works especially well if you can find a pattern or a logical way to organize the information. For example, let's say you meet a lot of relatives at a family reunion. You could try to remember each family as a group.

Or, you could make groups of the little kids, kids your own age, teenagers, adults, and elders.

Let's say you need to remember a number. Think about typing the number on a keyboard. What pattern would it form? You might be able to remember the pattern better than the number itself.

1st try

5th try

12th try

## Practice

Pay attention to the things around you. Note what people are wearing, and then try to remember it later. You can also set up tests for yourself or among your family and friends. For example, have someone put a dozen objects on a tray. Take two minutes to memorize what you see and then hide the tray. Try to list or draw all the objects. You can also do this with a list of written words or numbers. Practice may not make perfection, but it does lead to improvement!

30th try

I'm getting pretty good at this!

Challenge your mind through games and puzzles. You can actually grow your brain in new ways by learning new skills, like playing an instrument or playing brain games. Look for games that make you pay attention and think.

## Did You Know?

Mnemonics are memory tricks that help people recall information better. One early study found that using mnemonic tricks helped students improve test scores by up to 77%! For instance, to remember the order of the eight planets (and Pluto the dwarf planet): My Very Educated Mother Just Served Us Nine Pizzas!

## Don't try too hard

Stress can make it harder to remember. If you're struggling, take a few deep breaths and remember to breathe using your stomach. Wait, your stomach has lungs?? Yep!

No, just kidding! You use your stomach muscles and diaphragm to expand your lungs. Think about something happy, like a waterfall of cookies, but healthy cookies!

As you relax, you might find it easier to remember. If you often feel anxious, seek help.

Before studying, set aside a few minutes for fun. Listen to a favorite song, play with a pet or take that pet for a walk, unless your pet is an eel! Relaxing helps relieve stress, so your brain is ready to learn.

### Tip!

It's easier to recall information in an environment similar to where you learned it. If you have to take a test in a classroom, seated at a desk, then study at a desk at home. Just don't bring your desk to school. That would be weird!

### Tip!

Sleep helps memories settle in your brain. Right before you go to sleep, spend a few minutes reviewing material you want to remember. When you wake up, test yourself on the material!

### Bonus!

You can keep your brain healthy through exercise, getting enough sleep, and eating healthy food! All the techniques in this book work together to keep your mind and body at their best!

### Tip!

Spread out your study time. If you're going to study five hours for a test, it's better to schedule five one-hour sessions over two or more days.

Taking regular breaks when you study is also helpful. The chemicals your brain needs for memory and attention get used up quickly. Doing the same activity for just ten minutes can use up these chemicals! Take a few minutes to stretch or walk around. Or try a different type of studying, such as singing or acting out your vocabulary words, or sketching a picture. After a quick break, your brain will be ready to create new memories again. Brains are cool that way!

Finally, you're more likely to remember something that is important to you. Before you tackle a new subject, think about why it is important. How might it help you in the future? How does it relate to other subjects? How does it relate to "real life"? Then, before you study, tell yourself and your brain that you want to remember what you're about to read!

Time to REMEMBER!

## What to do:

Do you want to improve your memory? Of course you do! This chapter had lots of ways to do that. First of all, make sure you're protecting your brain during sports and athletic activities. Avoiding head injuries is one of the most important things you can do to keep your brain healthy.

We've got LoTS of options!

## Tip!

It's hard to start new habits. You might want to begin by using reminders. Set up a reminder on any device, or put a calendar somewhere that you can see. Use that as a reminder to practice your memory techniques. Basically, the hardest part is remembering to remember!

The next thing you can do is review the section on techniques for improving your memory. Don't try everything at once. That's kind of like using every power up in a video game at once! It's not really going to help you any more than just using one would. You probably wouldn't be able to remember all the things that were supposed to help you remember! Instead, choose one technique to try. Spend a week or two building up a new habit. After that, you can try adding another new habit. Over time, you'll find the memory aids that you like and that help you the best.

Your brain is like any other muscle: the more you use it, the better it will develop. Actually, it is WAY stronger than any other muscle, because each neuron can grow thousands of connections!

## A healthy and compassionate world

Our book is focused on health, but we're also very passionate about animals and the environment. Today, most food animals are raised in Concentrated Animal Feeding Operations (CAFO). CAFOs are also called factory farms. At a CAFO, tens of thousands of animals are packed close together. They may be kept in tiny cages. This is not kind to the animals because in these confined spaces, they live their entire lives under stress and continuous suffering. Factory farms also cause damage to the environment. They occupy large areas of land, which have to be deforested in order to make space for factory farms. They produce huge amounts of manure, which get can get into local rivers and streams. This can kill fish and make local water unsafe to drink. They are one of the leading sources of greenhouse gases that is contributing to climate change. Factory farms also use a lot of chemicals, and these chemicals can poison the soil and local water systems. A plant-based diet is the single biggest way to reduce your impact on our planet by reducing greenhouse gases, land use and water use.

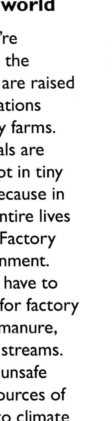

## Learn more

The organization Mercy For Animals fights cruelty to animals. This includes farm animals. See how you can help at mercyforanimals. org. The Humane Society of the United States publishes three bi-monthly magazines: All Animals for members, Animal Sheltering for shelter and rescue professionals, and Kind News for kids. Learn more at www. humanesociety.org.

## Chapter 2: True or False Answers

1. People only use 10 percent of their brain.

   False. There may be times when you are only using 10 percent of your brain, but most of the brain is active most of the time. Over the course of a day, you use 100 percent of your brain. Yes, everybody uses 100 percent of their brain, even your cousin Frank who still thinks the world is flat.

2. We are either "left brain" logical people or "right brain" creative people.

   False. Everyone uses both sides of the brain for every brain activity. Weird side note: there are people who have severe brain issues and the only way to fix them is to remove one half of the brain! Luckily, the other half of the brain can take over the responsibilities of the removed half so they can live normally! That's awesome!

I think...
Therefore:
I AM COOL!

Blind person            Seeing person

3. Female and male brains are different, so girls and boys learn differently.

   Partially true, but mostly false. There are some differences in female and male brains, however, the variations are small and don't make a big difference in learning. Also, there's a lot of overlap, so many boys and girls are just the same. Basically, there's no reason to teach children any differently.

4. We each have a different learning style. Some people learn better visually and some learn better by hearing the material aloud.

   Unknown. For all the talk about different learning styles, we haven't found any evidence to prove its true, yet! Maybe YOU will be the scientist who figures it out!

5. People can sometimes recover from brain damage.

   True, the brain can recover from some injuries, but not all brain damage can be healed. A lot of times, even if the brain doesn't heal, it can compensate for damage. As mentioned before, people have had parts of their brains removed and still lived normal lives.

6. A blind person maybe able to hear better than the average person.

   True. When one sensory input area isn't used, other's may improve. Someone who is blind may have more growth in the parts of the brain responsible for hearing or tbouch. Then, their sensitivity to sounds, or touch, or maybe both, are stronger.

# Chapter 3
# Eat Healthy

**True or False**

1. Sugar is bad for you.

2. Salt is bad for you.

3. Fat is bad for you.

4. A plant-based diet is always healthy.

5. Caffeine gives you energy!

6. You can propel a rocket with your burps! Okay, we can answer that one now. No, you can't really do that. Or, well, maybe a really small rocket?

Find the answers at the end of the chapter.

## How food affects your brain

Your brain works 24 hours a day, even when you're asleep. Your brain needs fuel, which comes from the foods you eat. Eating healthy foods makes for a healthy brain.

Foods can cause or decrease inflammation throughout the body. Inflammation is a defense mechanism by your body towards injury or infection. If you twist your ankle, you might get inflammation around the ankle. But eating the wrong foods can increase inflammation where you don't need it.

Eating junk food might make you feel good for a few minutes (and nothing wrong with that on rare occasions), but eating healthy foods can make you feel better in body and mind for much longer.

Our brain is always producing waste that is cleared by cells that serve as the maintenance unit - like janitors. This garbage in the brain is known as free radicals, which can cause slowing of the brain and damage to the structure of the brain. Imagine a building covered with trash - if the mess isn't cleaned up, the walls and floors will erode, the electrical wiring will be damaged, and you can just forget about moving quickly through that building!

Of course, if there's waste, the janitor has to clean it. Antioxidants are the janitors of the brain! Antioxidants, which are found mostly in plants, are chemicals that repair damage in our bodies and most importantly in the brain. Antioxidants are found in the color of the fruits, vegetables, whole grains and beans. The more color a plant has, the more antioxidants it has.

# What is a healthy diet?

Your diet refers to the food you eat. Some people are confused about what's good and what's bad for them. You can find a lot of advice about diet and nutrition. There is so much information out there and some advice might disagree with other advice. It really is hard to keep up with what's true and what's just a fake. Here's what's been proven so far (based on scientific research on thousands and thousands of people over decades):

A plant-based diet that is high in vegetables, fruits, beans, lentils, nuts, seeds, and whole grains is the healthiest diet. It's important to eat these in their whole, unprocessed form, because they contain all the carbohydrates, proteins, fats, vitamins and minerals that our body needs, and can absorb and use. For example, a grape is a whole food in its original state. Raisins are moderately processed grapes - they've been dried. Grape juice is highly processed. It may have added sugar and other ingredients. Fiber and some nutrients may have been removed. Grape juice might not even include much of the original grape. It could even be completely fake - a mix of sugar and artificial flavor. The unprocessed grape is healthier because it has lots of fiber, vitamins, minerals, and powerful chemicals called antioxidants.

Age 10 → Age 20 → Age 40

Note: Many plant foods like sour cherries can signficantly reduce inflammation!

The types of foods that are bad for the brain are the ones that are made from processed sugar, like soda, candies, donuts, cakes and cookies, fast foods that are fried, salty, processed, and animal protein and fats like beef, pork, bacon, chicken, turkey, eggs and dairy.

 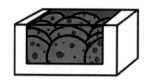  

Children who are raised on a plant-based diet will have a lower risk of heart disease, stroke, diabetes, cancer, and many other diseases related to obesity compared to other kids raised on the average American diet heavy in the stuff listed above. Because of this, they will also tend to live much longer.

## But what about protein?

Our brain and bodies need protein to grow, but the protein we get from whole grains, beans, nuts, seeds and vegetables are plenty. No one in the U.S. suffers from protein shortage. That usually happens in places where the children don't have access to food, and are starving. So protein deficiency is extremely unlikely on a diet drawn from a variety of plant foods.

## What about vitamins and minerals?

You can get all your vitamins from a whole food plant-based diet. But make sure your plate is full of many colors, as the more types of fruits and vegetables on your plate, the more likely that you have covered all the vitamins.

Calcium is an important mineral that helps our bones and our brains! We can get plenty of calcium from beans, green vegetables, including collards, kale, broccoli, mustard greens, swiss chard, and sweet potatoes. When we eat a lot of fruits and vegetables and avoid salty foods, our bodies retain more calcium!

Iron can be found in beans, green leafy vegetables, and nuts and seeds. The vitamin C in vegetables and fruits help to absorb iron better, so if we add some salsa (tomatoes and lemon juice have a lot of vitamin C) to a bean burrito (rich in iron), we're pumping iron in our bodies!

## What about fat?

Fats are not bad. It's the type of fat that matters. The type of fat that is good for the brain comes from - drumroll - plants! Think nut butters, seeds, avocados, and olives. However, since fats have a lot of calories, we have to make sure we eat it in small amounts only.

The fats that are not healthy are 'trans fats' found in junk foods, 'saturated fats' and 'cholesterol found in animal products. These types of fats clog the arteries that supply oxygen to our brain - think of a massive block on the highway (your blood vessels) that takes glucose and oxygen to different parts of the brain. If we build healthy habits during childhood, we'll have the best brains when we grow up!

Whole grains are edible plants that grow like grass. Wheat, rice, oats, quinoa, and corn are common grains. We don't usually eat grain in a completely natural state. Usually, we eat grains in foods such as bread, breakfast cereals, or pasta. Foods made 100% from whole grains use the entire kernel of the grain (think of whole wheat bread). Refined grains have the healthy part of the kernel removed (think of white bread). It also removes some important nutrients in the process.

## Did You Know?

One in 3 children in the U.S. is overweight or suffer from obesity! Obesity can lead to a lot of diseases in adulthood if it is not controlled.

They also don't have as much fiber as whole grains. Fiber is important for good brain health because it gives vitamins and minerals and helps your body get rid of all the garbage (basically, it helps you poop), and most of us don't get enough of it.

So, whole grains are less processed, and are healthier than refined grains!

Brown rice is healthier than white rice, because brown rice has the whole grain. White rice has been processed. Similarly, bread made from 100% whole wheat is healthier than white bread. So what about a cookie made with white flour, sugar, butter, and other ingredients? It's getting even farther away from the original wheat plant. And, as you can probably guess, it's not healthy at all. Still, there are times when you just hear a cookie calling to you. Go for it! There's nothing wrong with a treat now and then, and you can learn how to make healthier cookies with whole wheat flour, dates, dark chocolate chips, walnuts, and nut butter!

Hopefully this is giving you an idea of how to identify healthy foods. If it's something you might grow in a garden, it should be healthy. If the food has a single ingredient, such as an apple or brown rice, it's probably healthier than something with lots of ingredients. These guidelines should help you figure out which foods are healthier. We don't want you to try to memorize long lists of 'good' or 'bad' foods. Just focus on whole, plant foods that have not been processed much. Your body and brain will thank you!

You can take a vitamin pill to get vitamins and minerals. However, it's better to get the nutrients you need from your food. Healthy foods have other important nutrients that are not found in pills. Don't depend on vitamins alone! A good rule of thumb is to eat at least five different colored fruits and veggies a day.

## Plant based eating

A plant-based diet can be very healthy, because vegetables are healthy. Kids eating more plants have lower risks of many diseases, including diabetes. Their immunity becomes stronger and they have less allergies, colds and other infections! On the other hand, potato chips are made of a plant, and a diet of nothing but potato chips would not be healthy at all, because potato chips are processed by being fried in bad fats. An unprocessed, or whole-food, plant-based diet is one with lots of vegetables, beans, nuts, fruits, and whole grains as unprocessed as possible. Michael Pollan, a famous author said, "If it came from a plant, eat it.; if it was made in a plant (factory), don't."

## Did You Know?

Americans eat more meat than almost anyone else in the world. The world average of meat consumption is about 92 pounds per year. Americans eat an average of 265 pounds of meat each year. Add in dairy products and eggs, and the average American eats over 900 pounds of animal products every year. This much meat eating has a huge consequence on our health as a nation as well as our environment as a planet.

## Is protein a problem?

Everyone needs protein, especially growing children and teenagers. You need protein to build muscles and to fight diseases and heal.

## Diet Through History

Neanderthals were a species of human that lived during the Ice Age, over 35,000 years ago. Some ate mainly fish, because they lived in snowy areas where they couldn't grow any food. Other groups ate a diet that was almost entirely plant-based. They also used medicines from plants to treat pain and sickness.

The ancient Romans used lead acetate to sweeten wine. Unfortunately for them, lead acetate is poisonous. Sooooo, they probably didn't have much fun after doing that!

The word 'diet' comes from the Greek word 'diaita'. But diaita described a way of life, not just what you ate. It included physical and mental health and how to live in society. Today, 'diet' refers to the kinds of food a person or animal usually eats. The word is also used for specific plans where some foods are restricted. Many people 'go on a diet' hoping to lose weight.

In the 1700s people ate on lead plates. After eating, a lot of them died. They blamed the deaths on tomatoes and thought they were poisonous! It turned out that lead is poisonous and that was killing them. A chef tried to poison Thomas Jefferson with a tomato soup in a bowl not made of lead. As you can guess, it didn't work.

Meat is one source of protein, but even if you don't eat meat, eating only plants will provide plenty of protein as well. It's found in many foods, such as nuts, seeds, beans, grains, soy, or even just vegetables. And some of the biggest animals you know of like elephants, gorillas, rhinos and many others, eat only vegetables and fruits. Basically, you don't need to worry about protein unless you're trying to win the world body-building championship at age 11!

## Carbohydrates: Energy source

There are three main categories of food: proteins, fats, and carbohydrates. All of these things are necessary. Our bodies need them to survive. Carbohydrates (or carbs) are the body's main source of energy. They are also important for brain function and affect your mood and memory. One study found that people on a low-carb diet had more depression, anxiety, and anger. Another study looked at women on a no-carb diet. They did worse on tests of brain function. So maybe keep those carbs in your diet, okay?

Carbohydrates are sugars, starches, and fibers. They can be found in fruits, vegetables, grains, and many other products. Carbohydrates are called either simple or complex. This refers to how quickly the sugar is digested. Simple carbs are easily digested, while complex carbs take longer to digest. Table sugar is a simple carb. Complex carbs are found in whole grains, beans, potatoes, nuts and fruits.

 **Amazing Animals!**

- The giant anteater has a tongue two feet long and saliva like glue. They can slurp up thousands of insects in a few minutes. Instead of teeth, they use hard growths on the inside of their mouths to grind up the food. They may also swallow small stones that help crush food in their stomachs.

- Leafcutter ants grow their own crops. They cut leaves using their jaws, carry the pieces back to the colony, and make a pile. Their feces (poop) and saliva help fertilize the leaves as they compost. This grows a fungus, which the ants then feed to their larva babies. Kind of like a gross circle of life.

- Some animals, like the Japanese macaque (snow monkey) wash their food before eating it!

**Tip!**

It's a good idea to eat small meals or healthy snacks every few hours. Regular, small amounts of healthy food provide a steady energy supply to your body.

Any of these carbs will provide energy. However, simple carbs give a quick boost of energy that quickly fades. Complex carbs provide energy that lasts longer. Complex carbs also tend to have more fiber and other helpful nutrients. For these and other reasons, it's better to eat complex carbs rather than simple carbs. The best diet contains a balance of proteins, fats, and more complex carbohydrates. These complex carbohydrates come from vegetables, fruits, and whole grains.

## Fat: the Good and the Bad

As we said earlier, there are good fats and bad fats, and we actually get way too much fat in our modern diet. Bad fats are the kind that block our blood vessels and also injure our cells. This bad kind of fat is called saturated fats.

There are also good fats that come from plants that are healthy, at least in appropriate amounts. These fats (poly- and mono-unsaturated fats - look for these on food labels) are necessary for our growth and we can get them from many sources, like olives, avocados, seeds and nuts.

Good Fats!

## The problem with sugar

Do you like sweets? Most people do. In prehistoric times, people needed all the sugar they could find because it was a quick source of energy, as they used a lot of energy hunting and gathering. Plus, the naturally sweet foods they found, such as fruits, were healthy.

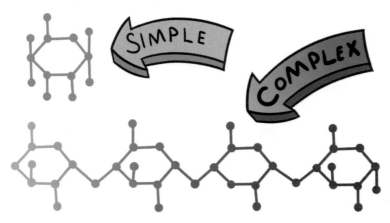

Here are the American Heart Association (AHA) recommendations for sugar:

- Children ages 4 to 8: no more than about 3 teaspoons (13 grams) of added sugar a day

- Pre-teen and teen kids: no more than 5 to 8 teaspoons (21 to 34 grams) a day

- Most adult women: no more than 6 teaspoons (25 grams) a day

- Most adult men: no more than 9 teaspoons (39 grams) a day

Ancient people around the world used honey or boiled grape juice to sweeten their foods, but for most of human history, people did not eat a lot of sweets. They couldn't get a lot of sweets. That's one of the reasons we crave sweet things. We've been programmed over hundreds of thousands of years to see sweets and think "Oh, that's hard to get! I better eat that now!"

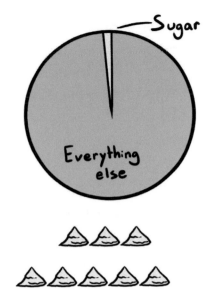

The discovery of sugar, made from sugarcane or sugar beets, changed that. Now sugar is cheap and you can find it in EVERYTHING. That makes it easy to eat too much of it. At the same time, we're no longer spending most of our time moving around outdoors. We don't need the energy to run away from lions anymore! Yet, our brains are all still very much like our ancestors who had to work hard for their sugar and even harder for their fats!

Scientists are still studying how sugar contributes to health problems. One thing we know: sugar has a lot of calories but little nutritional value. Eating a lot of sugar can mean you don't get enough healthy foods. Or it may mean you're eating too many calories overall. This can cause weight gain, and obesity increases the risk of heart disease, diabetes and depression, among other problems. Sugar is sometimes called 'empty calories'. This means that eating sugar means eating a bunch of calories with no nutrients. We don't think it's empty, though. Sugar robs us of our brain function and our health. It's worse than empty. We prefer to think of sugar as toxic calories.

Many manufactured foods also have sugar - often a lot of it. You might also add other sweeteners to your food. Most people don't realize how much sugar they consume from all these sources. The average adult eats about 22 teaspoons of sugar every day. About a third of this sugar comes from soft drinks. They're called soft drinks because drinking too many of them makes your tummy soft. Other big sources are fruit drinks, candies, cookies, and other sweets. Some juices can have 10-20 teaspoons of sugar in one serving!

## How much is too much?

Most experts say we should have very little sugar. In fact, you don't need any added sugar. You do need sugar, but we get all we need from complex carbs.

Guess how many teaspoons of sugar are in a 12 ounce can of soda? Ten! That means drinking a single can of soda provides way too much sugar in a day, no matter what your age. You're literally overdosing on a snack! And diet sodas have so many other weird chemicals as well!

So it's best to drink water, or fruit smoothies if you like sweetness. It's hard to cut out all sugar, but try reducing the amount you take in. Look for the high-sugar foods in your diet. Can you eat or drink something else instead? Fresh and dried fruit make a nice, sweet snack.

## How sweet is it?

You probably know that candy bars are high in sugar. But it's not always easy to tell when a food has a lot of sugar. For example, breakfast cereal can have a little, or a lot, or way too much, all depending on the type. The trick is to read the labels on the back of your food!

## Better snacking

When you're hungry, it may be tempting to reach for cookies, candy, or other junk food. Here are some snack options that are better for your body and brain:

- Fruit: Bananas, apples, oranges, grapes, kiwis, berries or other fruit

- Veggies: Carrots, broccoli, cauliflower, celery, cucumber slices, etc. Enjoy them by themselves or with nut butter or hummus

- Nuts and seeds, or trail mix with nuts, seeds, and dried fruit

- Whole-grain breakfast cereal with almond milk

- Unsweetened applesauce

- Oat bars or healthy muffins make with whole grains, nuts and fruits

## Did You Know?

Just because something is 'natural' does not mean it's healthy. Many sweeteners are very similar, chemically speaking. In fact, most types of sugars or sweeteners aren't that different, whether they're natural or not, and a 'natural' sugar can act just like regular white sugar and can be as harmful. Also, there's no legal definition of natural. That means something labeled 'natural' could be harmful. Well, dirt is very natural, but you probably don't want to eat dirt!

## Sugar by any name tastes sweet

Sugar is a simple carbohydrate. Sucrose, glucose, fructose, and lactose are the main types of sugar. Sucrose comes from sugar cane, sugar beets, and a few other plants. Glucose is found in many plant foods.

Many fruits and some vegetables contain fructose. Other natural sweeteners are agave and maple syrup. Agave and maple syrup contain equal amounts of fructose and glucose. Cornstarch can also be made into a sweetener. On food labels, this may be called high fructose corn syrup, corn sugar, crystalline fructose, dextrose, or maltodextrin. Don't worry! You don't have to remember all those names! Just remember, sugar can have many names, so you may be getting more sugar than you realize. And second, there is little nutritional difference between these sweeteners.

## Sugar addiction

When sugar touches your taste buds, they send a pleasure signal to the brain. Your brain responds by wanting to eat more sugar. Sugar also affects the hormones that tell the brain if you're hungry. With sugar, the more you eat, the less your brain realizes you've had enough. Eating sugar makes you want more sugar. Some scientists think sugar can be addictive. Someone with an addiction cannot control what they're eating, using, or taking. Some scientists believe that sugar can make you lose control just like addictive drugs do. Once again, this probably all dates back to our ancient ancestors who would 'see food, eat food' because high energy foods were hard to find.

## Weird and Wacky!

People have tried some pretty crazy diets over the years. A 'fad diet' is one that makes big promises, usually about losing weight. These diets may cause a quick weight loss, but they don't last. The diet industry companies that sell books, programs, or special foods for dieters is a huge business. People spend millions of dollars every year on these products. This has led to some pretty weird and dangerous diets.

- Fletcherism was a diet where you had to chew your food for a long time. One bite might be chewed 700 times!

- The early 1900s brought the tapeworm diet. Dieters would swallow a pill with tapeworm larva. These parasites grow up to 30 feet long. They absorbed food in the intestines but a caused many illnesses. Health 101: PLEASE DON'T EAT PARASITES!!!

- Diet pills and potions made big promises, but they often had dangerous ingredients.

- Poisons such as arsenic and strychnine would be added. Dozens of people have died from taking diet products.

- Some people have literally tried to starve themselves thin. The Breatharian Diet asked people to live on air alone - no food of any kind.

## Fun Fact!

You don't get nutrients from air!

**Amazing Animals!**

- Humans, of course, use many tools to get and prepare food. Some other animals also use tools to get at their food. Many animals use rocks on nuts, fruits, or shellfish, to break open hard shells. Some use sticks or stone tools to dig for vegetables, insects, or worms.

- The Egyptian vulture loves ostrich eggs. To break one open, it picks up rocks in its beak and throws them at the egg. Ostriches are not big fans of vultures!

- The bolas spider throws a ball of its silk at an insect to catch it. Maybe that's where Spiderman got the idea for his web shooters?

- The New Caledonian crow catches prey on hooks made out of twigs.

- Chimpanzees make spears out of wood for hunting. Don't mess with Chimps!

- People claim to have seen polar bears throw large chunks of ice at their prey to kill it. Maybe that's where the phrase, "putting them on ice" comes from?

## Hint!

No diet will work unless it comes with complete lifestyle changes. These are things that you can do in your everyday life that helps you. The best way to diet is to eat a bit less food and more vegetables, which have much fewer calories that you'll be able to use! Calories that you don't use right away get stored as fat.

## Did You Know?

Different animals have different numbers of taste buds. Humans have approximately 10,000 taste buds. Chickens only have about 30. Cows have around 25,000 and catfish have more than 100,000! Taste buds help animals identify poisons or spoiled food. An animal that's more likely to be near poisons than other animals will have more taste buds to identify more poisons.

Uh...

Dehydration

## What to drink

Your body needs water in order to function. In fact, 70% of your body is made of water. If you don't drink enough liquids, you can suffer from dehydration. Dehydration happens when more water leaves your body than you take in. You lose water through sweating, urinating, and even through breathing. You probably won't notice how much water you're losing, so dehydration can sneak up on you.

At first you might feel thirsty. You might not need to pee as much, and your urine might be darker. Over time, dehydration can cause lightheadednness, muscle cramps, and other symptoms.

Dehydration affects your brain as well. If you don't get enough water, your brain actually shrinks! Nobody wants a shrunken brain!

Some studies even say that dehydrated people have worse brain function. Drinking water may not literally make you smarter, but it does let you use your brain to its full extent!

It's a good idea to drink a glass of water when you get up in the morning. That will help replace water you lost while you slept. Make sure you drink some with meals, and maybe in between meals. You may have heard you should 'drink eight glasses of water each day', but there's no scientific evidence that eight glasses is the exact right amount. Still, it's a good target. Larger people probably need more water than smaller ones. If you exercise or sweat a lot from heat, you'll need to drink extra. Does it have to be water? No, any sugar-free beverage counts.

However, we recommend water because it does not have calories, sugar, or artificial ingredients. If you don't like plain water, try sparkling water or add some fruit, a squirt of lemon or lime juice, or a slice of orange or cucumber. Yum!

Frozen grapes or strawberries can keep a drink cold and add a bit of flavor. You can also try drinking water at different temperatures. Maybe you'll prefer room temperature instead of ice cold, or maybe the reverse!

Caffeine may give you a quick mental boost, but it's definitely not a healthy way to get one. It can be harmful for kids!

## What to do

Keep a food diary. Note what you eat and how you feel after eating it. Pay attention to how you feel later in the day, and the next day as well. For the first week or two, stick to the pattern you already have. How does it make you feel? Then, try to eat a whole food, plant-based diet. Cut out or reduce processed foods and sugar. Make sure you're eating plenty of healthy foods instead. How do you feel on this diet?

If cutting out all sugar and processed foods sounds too painful, start smaller. Choose one unhealthy food to cut from your diet. For example, you might start by switching from soda to fruit smoothies or water. Try making another healthy change every 2-4 weeks. You can also try leaving other foods out of your diet entirely. Some people feel better if they don't eat dairy products such as milk and cheese. You might try each of these diets for two or three weeks. What works best for you?

It can be hard to eat a diet you're not used to. It takes some planning and preparation. It's easier if your entire family is eating the same thing. Ask your family members to read this chapter, and see if they're willing to try these different foods together. You can encourage each other to eat healthy. You can stop buying junk food while testing the new diet. It's easier to follow through on your goals if you don't have a lot of temptation sitting around. It's also easier if you have supportive and encouraging people around you.

Be sure to help out planning menus, making shopping lists, and preparing food. You're responsible for your own health, so don't expect someone else to do all the work!

# Chapter 3
# Review!

## Chapter 3: True or False Answers

1. Sugar is bad for you.

   True. Sugar is linked to many health problems. Many Americans consume way too much sugar.

2. Too much salt is bad for you.

   True. High levels of salt can be very bad for some people. We rarely have problems with too little salt because all our foods have plenty of salt or sodium in them.

3. Fat is bad for you.

   Partly True. We need some fat in our diet, but it's the type of fat that matters. Fats that come from plants like peanut butter, nuts, seeds, avocados, and olives are okay in small amounts. But animal fats, like cholesterol, saturated fats, and trans fats are not healthy. Many Americans get far more animal fats than they need. Too much can cause health problems.

4. A vegetarian diet is always healthy.

   False. A vegetarian diet can be very healthy, but just because something is vegetarian does not make it healthy. Like everyone else, vegetarians should mainly eat healthy foods like vegetables and not unhealthy foods like candy, fries, and soda.

5. Caffeine gives you energy.

   True, but caffeine can give you a short energy burst, but it doesn't last long. Caffeine also has harmful effects, especially for kids. It can really affect attention and focus in a negative way. There are better ways to improve your energy!

# Chapter 4
# Exercise

**True or False**

1. Exercise can make you smarter.

2. All forms of exercise are the same.

3. Exercise can give you a natural "high", a boost in mood.

4. You need to exercise every day to be healthy.

5. You can't exercise too much.

6. When girls do jumping jacks they're called jumping jills. (Okay, just checking to make sure you're paying attention. That's definitely not true!)

Find the answers at the end of the chapter.

## Why we exercise

Exercise is good for your entire body. It can help you keep healthy and avoid diseases. Some exercises strengthen your muscles, while others make you more flexible. Exercise can improve your stamina, so you have more energy, and it can even make you feel happier!

There are four basic types of exercise: aerobic, strength, balance, and flexibility. Each of these types are important. Some sports and activities fit all four categories, while others fit fewer categories. Ideally you want to do different exercises that help you develop in all four areas.

**Bonus!**

Some people claim that you shouldn't exercise close to bedtime. This may be true for some people. If you have this problem, try to finish your exercise a couple of hours before bedtime. A study showed that most people were not affected by exercising right before bedtime. A poll of 1,000 people found that most people sleep better on days they exercise.

## Exercise Throughout History

In ancient times, activity was part of daily life. People walked to visit neighboring tribes. Hunting and gathering food required physical fitness. Our ancestors had to go find their food so they were always on the move. Even entertainment, such as dancing and games, kept people moving.

As societies became more civilized, people became more sedentary. A sedentary person is someone who is not physically active. More people started to have health problems related to a lack of fitness.

Track and field events have also been around for centuries. The ancient Greeks and Romans practiced running, jumping, and throwing the javelin and discus. Archery and fencing were other popular sports.

For much of human history, women were not allowed to participate in sports. One form of exercise was developed for women in the 1500's. It was calisthenics (gymanstic exercises) performed with music.

Even running was seen as a man's sport until fairly recently. Many people thought women were too frail to run, or that running would damage them. Today, experts agree that running and other sports are perfectly healthy for girls and women.

# Aerobic exercise

With aerobic exercise, you quickly move your larger muscle groups such as your legs and arms. Think of walking, jogging, bicycling, or swimming. These activities get your heart beating faster, moving blood throughout your body. Your lungs also work harder, so you breathe more quickly and deeply. Aerobic means "with oxygen", and these exercises help your body use oxygen.

These forms of fitness are sometimes called cardio. Cardio is short for cardiovascular exercise. It refers to any exercise that raises your heart rate. Actually, almost any exercise will raise your heart rate. Getting out of bed in the morning will raise your heart rate! Calling an exercise cardio or aerobic usually means it speeds up your heart beat a lot. You may also hear the term endurance, because the activity endures (lasts) for a long time at a steady pace.

Aerobic exercise is great for your health. It boosts your immune system, so you can fight sickness better. You are less likely to get colds and the flu. Regular aerobic exercise can help you maintain a healthy weight. This, along with the exercise itself, lowers your risk of many health problems. Heart disease, blood pressure, type 2 diabetes, and even ADHD (Attention Deficit Hyperactivity Disorder) or ADD (Attention Deficit Disorder) might sound like problems for adults. Well, they can affect young people as well, but exercise helps these conditions. Plus, developing healthy habits now will make it easier to stay healthy for the rest of your life.

Aerobic exercise is good for your body, but it's also good for your brain as well. It can reduce stress and nervousness and boost self-esteem. People who exercise regularly have lower rates of depression. Exercise also increases energy levels. This may be because aerobic exercise releases special chemicals.

Some of these chemicals are natural pain killers that make you feel good. They can help your body learn how to deal with stress.

Aerobic exercise may even make you smarter. At least, it can help you use your brain better. Chemicals released during exercise can actually improve brain health, especially memory. Exercise can help your brain grow new neurons (nerve cells that carry messages between the brain and other parts of the body).

Exercise brings more blood flow to the pre-frontal cortex of the brain. That's the part that helps control behavior. With more activity there, it's easier to think before you act. In other words, it helps you do fewer silly things by accident. You may be able to focus and pay attention better. Plus, after burning off some energy, you may feel calmer and find it easier to behave. It turns out there are lots of reasons to get into aerobic exercise.

Any exercise that makes your heart beat faster and your lungs work harder to breathe is likely aerobic. If you are moving a lot, that's a good sign an activity is aerobic. A wide variety of sports and activities are aerobic. Team sports, such as soccer or basketball, where you run a lot, also count as aerobic. You can also do aerobic activities such as hiking or jogging by yourself or with a few friends.

### Tip!
Be sure to drink plenty of water before, during, and after strenuous exercise. When you work out, you lose water by sweating and even by breathing. This can lead to dehydration, a harmful loss of water from the body, and make you very sick

### Bonus!
You can find out if you're drinking enough by weighing yourself before and after exercise. If you lose weight during a workout, that shows you are losing more water (through sweat) than you're taking in (by drinking). In other words, you're NOT drinking enough.

### Hint!
If you're not peeing enough, you most likely also aren't drinking enough water. Look, people, you NEED water, so DRINK!

Water is your friend!

Drink!
Drink!
Drink!!

Drinking plenty of water means you can work out longer and feel better. Yet most athletes don't drink enough. You should be drinking water throughout the day. An hour or so before you plan to work out, drink an extra one or two glasses. Drink another glass about 15 minutes before you begin. As you are working out, drink about eight ounces every 15 minutes. If you're sweating a lot, you should drink even more - and shower afterwards, your family will thank you!

## Get outdoors

Exercise is especially good for your brain if you're out in nature! One study compared people who hiked in a natural environment with those who hiked in a city. People who walked in nature had fewer negative thoughts.

Of course, that could be just from less horns honking at them. Another study sent people on a backpacking trip without any technology. Their ability to solve problems improved by 50%! It may be that getting away from the noise and distractions of a city made it easier to focus.

And, of course, leaving your electronic devices at home gets rid of that distraction. You might want to consider doing some time each day without your electronics. For the first millions of years of humanity, our ancestors survived with no electronic devices. So you can probably make it an hour or so!

As another bonus, people who exercise outside are more likely to keep doing the activity. If you can't get out in the wilderness, try a park or riverside trail, or even a big backyard picnic!

## Strength training

Strength exercises build up strong muscles. They also help build muscle endurance. Muscle strength helps you lift heavy things. Endurance helps you hold a weight for a longer time. Strength training also helps strengthen the tendons that connect muscles to bones, and the ligaments that connect the bones in you joints. Strength training even improves bone density, literally building stronger bones. Strong bones are great for holding big muscles.

Guess what? Strength training is good for your brain, too. You guessed it, didn't you? Several studies have shown that older adults who do strength training have better brain function. In fact, people who did weight training had healthier brains than those who just did special brain training. Maybe weights should be called Smartbells instead of Dumbbells?

Weightlifting is a clear example of strength training. With weightlifting, you lift weights such as dumbbells and barbells, or use weight machines in a gym.

Weight training is safe for children aged eight or older, but you should be trained by an experienced adult. Your focus should be on getting stronger, not on building large muscles. For children and teens, experts recommend using light weights. Don't use weights that are so heavy you can only lift them a few times. Instead, use lighter weights and do more repetitions.

When you're first learning strength training, try the exercises without any extra weight. It's way more important to learn the proper form. If you're twitching, flailing, or flinging your weights around, the weight is probably too heavy and you could hurt yourself or the people around you. You should always feel in control.

It's best to do weight training no more than three times a week. Warm up with some easy aerobic exercise and stretching. Use light weights and do 8-10 repetitions. Do some more gentle stretching when you're finished with the weight training. As you get stronger, you can do more repetitions of each exercise, or use slightly heavier weights. Many sports build up your muscles. For example, running and cycling mainly use (and build) the leg muscles. Swimming and ballet, on the other hand, use muscles throughout the entire body.

## Did You Know?

Some athletes use steroids to build muscles. This is illegal and dangerous!

## Balance

Good balance can help you avoid falls and move more easily. Balance is controlled through signals to the brain from other parts of your body, including your eyes and ears. Without balance, you couldn't even walk across the room. Sports and athletic activities require balance, so they build balance as you do them. Plus, strong muscles make it easier to balance, so any activity that builds muscles will help your balance.

Certain exercises are especially good for building balance. Tai Chi is a gentle, slow-moving martial art that is great for balance and relaxation. You can even do simple balance exercises standing around your house. Try balancing on one leg to start. How long can you do it? Look up "balance exercises" online for more ideas.

Flexibility means "able to bend or be bent, usually without breaking". In case you didn't know, breaking people is bad. In exercise, flexibility is the ability to move through a range of motion. This can help you in many sports and physical activities. Good flexibility can also help you avoid injuries. Yep, practicing your bending can help you avoid breaking. You've heard of 'what bends doesn't break', right?

### Tip!

If you have a lot of trouble with balance, you may have a health problem. If your balance suddenly grows worse, or if you have unusually bad balance, talk to a doctor.

Your brain also benefits from stretching. Studies show that stretching can help your memory and may help you think more clearly. It can also improve your mood. If you're crabby, maybe try a few stretches. Stretching works with the other three types of exercise to build a strong body and a healthy mind.

You build flexibility by stretching your muscles. Yoga is a great way to do this. You can also do a variety of simple stretching exercises at home. Look up "stretching exercises" or "flexibility exercises" for instructions. Here are some basic guidelines:

- Warm up before stretching. Try taking a brisk walk to get your blood moving and your muscles loosened. You can also stretch after your athletic activity.

- Don't lock your joints (elbows and knees) in a straight position. Your joints should always be slightly bent.

- Stretch until you feel a bit tense, and then hold it there. At first, you might hold it about 10 seconds. As you get better, you can hold each pose for 30 and then 60 seconds. Don't bounce, and don't stretch too far. If you feel numbness, tingling, or more than mild pain, you've gone too far. In other words, STOP!

- Breathe deeply and slowly as you stretch!

Note: You can even make taking out the trash a nice exercise! By lifting it up and down as you walk. Just don't spill the trash! And the same goes for groceries!

## Getting started

For the best body and brain health, find activities you enjoy that give you all four kinds of exercise. Try to do them several days a week. Taking a class or joining a team can be a great way to learn a new sport or activity. You may also be able to find workout videos or instructions online.

These are general guidelines. How you do an exercise can make a difference. For example, yoga almost always builds balance and flexibility. It can also be aerobic if it's done quickly, or muscle-building if some difficult poses are used. Ballet uses muscles throughout the body, while other forms of dance may primarily the lower body. Think about what you've learned about the four types of exercise. You can probably figure out how different activities fit. After all, you're super smart!

## How much is enough?

Try to exercise for at least 20 to 30 minutes at a time. It's great if you can do this every day, but even a few times a week will help. If you have not been exercising, start out slowly. It might seem hard at first, but it will get easier if you exercise regularly. At first you could try speed walking for 20 minutes three times a week. After a few weeks, increase the amount of time you walk, or your speed. You can also start exercising more days per week. Try some different exercises, such as bicycling or swimming, to see what you enjoy the best. Variety is good because it works your body in different ways. It also helps keep things interesting! You'll be more likely to keep the healthy practice if you enjoy it!

Daily exercise is a great habit! However, it is possible to exercise too much. Your body needs time to heal from the physical stress exercise causes. Exercising too much, especially doing the same exercise every day, can lead to injuries. You could tear muscles or break bones! Ouch!

Experts generally suggest you only do an activity five days a week at the most. During your days off, you can try a different activity. In other words, it's okay to exercise every day, but avoid doing the same exercise every day. If you have a favorite activity, think about what you can do in your days off to keep your body in balance. For example, if you usually run, you're doing a great workout for your heart, lungs, and legs. A couple days a week, try doing some yoga instead to work on your balance and flexibility. Or go for a swim! Also, if you play a team sport, experts suggest taking off two or three months a year. Try another activity during those months!

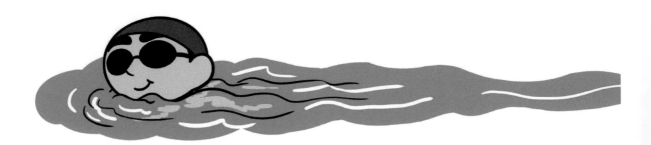

# Weird and Wacky

Sometimes people get bored doing the same old exercise year after year. That's why people have invented some cool forms of exercise!

Aerial yoga, or anti-gravity yoga, uses hammocks or slings hung from the ceiling. People can do moves while hanging upside down. That's why we call it Spiderman yoga! It's combined with trapeze. There are also anti-gravity ballet classes using the same kind of equipment. Some gyms even offer circus workouts that include acrobatics and trapeze. Let's hope they use a net!

Reverse running doesn't require any special equipment. Running backwards uses different muscles and improves balance. But it's also easier to trip or crash into things, and your neighbors may give you funny looks.

## What to do

You'll find it easier to stick with exercise if you can find exercises you enjoy. So what's right for you?

- Do you have any health conditions that affect how much you can and should exercise?

- Do you have restrictions on what you can do? If the answer is yes or maybe, consult with your doctor.

- Would you rather exercise alone, with a friend or two, or in a large group?

- Do you enjoy competition?

- Do you prefer to set your own schedule or have a regular meeting time?

- What times are best for you?

- What activities are available to you? What can your family afford?

- How much time can you spend? That can be a big factor!

Ask for advice if you need help understanding what an activity involves or what's healthy for you. You might talk to your doctor, school nurse, gym teacher or coach.

Then try out some sports or exercise routines. You may need to try something a few times before deciding if you like it. It takes time to learn new skills so don't get discouraged if you're not good right away. Focus on learning and having fun!

# Chapter 4
# Review!

### Chapter 4: True or False Answers

1. Exercise can make you smarter.

   True. Hormones released during exercise are linked to improved memory. Memory isn't quite the same thing as intelligence, but being able to remember things can help with many mental tasks.

2. All forms of exercise are the same.

   False. There are four basic kinds of exercise: aerobic, strength training, balance, and flexibility. All types are beneficial to our bodies and minds.

3. Exercise can give you a natural "high", a boost in mood.

   True. Exercise releases natural painkillers that make you feel good. Exercising regularly can lower stress and anxiety as well.

4. You need to exercise every day to be healthy.

   False. It's a good idea to exercise every day. However, you do not need to do a hard workout every single day. It's okay to rest once in a while, especially if you're sick or injured. Aim to get some exercise at least five days a week.

5. You can't exercise too much.

   False. Exercising too much can cause injuries.

# Chapter 5
# Sleep Well

**True or False**

1. We need sleep, just like we need food and water.

2. We spend one quarter of our lives asleep.

4. Scientists don't really know why we sleep.

5. Staying up late to study will make you smarter the next day.

6. Sheep sleep 23.5 hours a day, and that's why people count them to go to sleep! Nope, still only checking to make sure you're paying attention! Critical thinking is important!

Find the answers at the end of the chapter.

# Why we sleep

After a good night's sleep, you should feel alert and energetic. Without enough sleep you are often slow and grumpy. But why do we need sleep at all? Scientists who study sleep have several theories.

One theory is that sleep keeps us safe at night. Humans don't have good night vision in the dark it's very easy to have accidents. Staying quiet and still at night also kept early humans safer from predators. This "inactivity theory" is also called the evolutionary theory of sleep. It says that we evolved to sleep at night so we would stay out of trouble.

Some people question that theory. When you're asleep, you don't know what's happening around you. Wouldn't it be safer to stay awake but lie quietly without moving? Have you ever had a sibling jump on you when you were asleep? DID YOU FEEL SAFE THEN?

Another theory says sleep helps us conserve energy. It's hard to hunt or gather food at night. Flashlights didn't exist for the first few million years! Fire for light doesn't exactly travel well! So why not sleep, and save our energy for daytime? People use as much as 10 percent less energy while they're sleeping. This is called the "energy conservation theory".

## Fun Fact!

Remember that an adult human brain weighs about three pounds. That's only about two percent of the average adult body weight. Yet the brain uses up to 25 percent of the body's energy! So yeah, the brain is an energy hog.

## Rest and restore

The "restorative theory" offers another answer. While you sleep, your muscles are growing and your tissues are repairing any damage. Growth hormone is released mostly during sleep. Bones seem to grow only during sleep. Muscles repair and grow while you sleep as well. It's hard for muscles and bones to grow while you're using them! Because children are still growing, they need more sleep than adults. Adults do need sleep too, because their bodies need a chance to repair any damage done during the day.

Your brain needs sleep, too. When you're awake and your brain is active, your brain makes something called adenosine. The levels of adenosine rise for every hour that you're awake. This substance does some good things in the body! It helps organs such as the heart and liver work well, but adenosine also depresses the central nervous system. Your central nervous system includes your brain and spinal cord. The nerves there control the activities in your body. When this system is depressed by adenosine, you get sleepy. When you sleep, your body clears the adenosine from your system. You wake up alert and ready for another day of action!

## Sleep to remember

Sleep also helps you learn. Getting a good night's sleep helps you remember the things you learned that day. Sleep allows your brain to form connections that become memories.

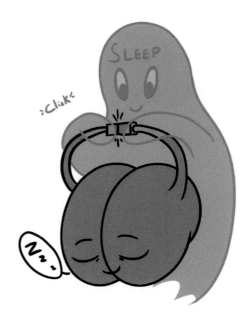

And sleep doesn't just help you remember facts, such as the state bird of California (it's the quail!). It helps you remember how to do things, like ride a bicycle, play an instrument, which T.V. stations have your favorite shows, or how to kick a soccer ball. Sleep helps you with everything you need or want to learn.

Your brain is like a storage room filled with information. When you want to remember something, you need to be able to find that information. Without enough sleep, it's hard to find the right information 'file'. It even becomes hard to make decisions. Making a good decision involves several steps: you have to understand the situation, look at the options, choose the right behavior, and act accordingly. Without enough sleep, it's hard to function!

Lack of sleep can even cause accidents. What happens if you're too tired to pay attention to what's happening around you? You're more likely to trip, drop something, or not see a person, object, or car heading toward you. Plus, tired muscles can't react as quickly. So, sleeping well can save your life!

## Lie down, cheer up

Being well-rested also helps you the next day. You've probably noticed how hard it is to pay attention when you're sleepy. Someone who does not get enough sleep is called sleep-deprived. If you're sleep-deprived, it's hard to focus and learn. How much you sleep can also affect your mood. Without enough sleep, you may be grumpy, and when you're grumpy, it's hard to do anything, learn new information, work on projects, play sports, make art or music, or even enjoy your own friends. And your friends won't think you're much fun to be around either!

Sleep is so important that animals forced to go without sleep die in a few weeks. They lose their immune function. Without immune function, the body cannot recognize and stop invaders such as viruses. This shows that we really do need sleep in order to restore the body. It also explains why you need more sleep when you're sick. Let's hope that our scientists are getting plenty of sleep so they can make big discoveries!

**Amazing Animals!**

- Giraffes sleep less than two hours every day, and they can go weeks without sleeping at all.

- Some birds will take hundreds of quick naps every day. These naps last only a few seconds while the bird is flying! Some types of birds will fly for six months straight, during migration. They eat, drink, and sleep, all while in the air.

- Other animals sleep many hours every day. Bats sleep for 20 hours a day while hanging upside down. Maybe Batman should have been Giraffeman, since they don't sleep, but that would be pretty ridiculous!

- Animals that live in water but breathe air have special tricks to sleep without drowning. Otters sleep while floating on their backs. Sometimes they hold paws with other otters to stay together. Some whales and seals only shut off part of their brain to sleep. The other half of their mind keeps working. This lets them stay near the surface of the water to breathe. Baby dolphins don't sleep at all during their few months of their life.

## Sleepy accidents

Some of the world's major accidents have been linked to sleep deprivation. These disaster happened when people in charge had to make important decisions while seriously sleep-deprived.

Exxon Valdez oil tanker spill: A ship ran aground near Alaska and spilled almost 11 million gallons of crude oil into the ocean. This devastated the environment! It affected many species of fish, birds, and sea mammals, such as otters and killer whales. Some animal species have still not fully recovered. This accident happened due to lack of sleep among people in charge.

Chernobyl nuclear meltdown: A nuclear power plant in Chernobyl, Ukraine, released radioactive poisons. More than 30 people died within a few weeks. More than 300,000 people had to move farther away from the accident site. In the following years, children in the surrounding areas got more cancer. This accident happened due to a lack of sleep.

Several factors played into each of these accidents. For example, the Chernobyl power plant did not have good safety procedures. Still, lack of sleep was a factor in each disaster.

So, could lives be saved if only everyone got enough sleep? Every year, more than 250,000 people because of medical errors. Many of those mistakes are related to doctors not getting enough sleep. Driving while tired is dangerous as well. At least 72,000 traffic accidents happen every year because of tired drivers. The bottom line is: Get Enough Sleep!

## Sweet dreams

There are two primary states of sleep. These are: rapid eye movement (REM) sleep, and non-rapid eye movement (NREM) sleep. Together, these stages make a sleep cycle. Each sleep cycle lasts about 90 minutes. In an average night, you have four to five sleep cycles. The brain behaves differently in REM sleep versus NREM sleep. REM sleep is a time for vivid dreams. During REM sleep, the brain is as active as when you're awake. On the other hand, muscles become completely paralyzed. The brain signals that control muscle movement are turned off. This may be a way of protecting you from acting out your dreams in the real world. Just imagine what would happen if we all acted out our dreams!

The eyes are the one exception to muscle action being stopped. REM sleep gets its name from the fact that the closed eyes move rapidly from side to side. It's cool and freaky at the same time. This apparently happens at random. We don't know exactly why, but the movement may be related to dreaming. During REM sleep, vivid dreams can cause brain waves to spike in parts of the brain involved with vision. So perhaps your eyes are 'seeing' your dreams using the back of your eyelids like a movie screen!

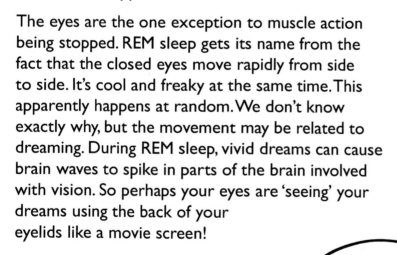

During REM sleep, your brain may practice the things you learned that day. Without REM sleep, it's harder to learn complex task. If you've had a few difficult days learning lots of new things, you may spend more time in REM sleep. Think of REM sleep as your brain's chance to do some filing. It can sort through what you learned that day and put that information in the right place.

During NREM sleep, the muscles are relaxed but not paralyzed. Meanwhile, the brain shows less activity. Think of this as your brain's chill out time! While REM sleep involves an active brain in a still body, NREM sleep involves a less active brain but moving body. If you wake up in a funny position, you probably shifted during NREM sleep. NREM sleep is when your body heals and repairs any damage. Toxins are cleared from the brain, leaving it healthier.

The amount of sleep you need depends on your age. Newborn babies need the most sleep - up to 14 to 17 hours a night. The number then starts dropping. Children age 6 to 13 should get 9 to 11 hours of sleep each night. Teenagers usually need 8 to 10 hours each night. Some people may need more or less sleep, but these numbers are appropriate for most of us.

Children, especially younger children, may not feel or act tired when they're sleepy. Instead, they get wound up and hyper. So if you feel like you really don't want to sleep- maybe you really should. You can be too tired to know you're tired!! How can you tell if you're getting enough sleep? Pay attention to how you feel during the day. If you get tired and cranky a lot, you may need more sleep.

## Can't sleep

Many adults suffer from sleep problems, but children can have them as well. In fact, one study found that 2/3 of children under age 10 have had some kind of sleep problem! These sleep problems can lead to bad grades, behavioral problems, and can make you sad and anxious.

Other sleep problems for children can include sleepwalking and night terrors. With sleepwalking, you may get up and move around while still asleep. During night terrors or sleep terrors, you might wake up in a paralyzed panic. It must be terrifying to wake up not being able to move. But, chances are, if you have these, they won't last for long! Practicing good sleep habits can help.

It's not unusual to have trouble sleeping for a night or two, but if the problem goes on for long, it can lead to many health problems, such as high blood pressure, diabetes and heart disease.

Sleeping too much is also associated with poor health or depression. If you sleep a lot and are still tired, talk to your doctor. In fact, if you have any kind of problem sleeping, and the 'Sleep Better' tips in this chapter don't work, you should talk to a doctor.

## Food, sleep, and weight

People who sleep less than six hours each night are more likely to be overweight. Among adults, those who sleep eight hours a night are the most likely to have a healthy weight. Remember, you need more sleep because you're still growing. During sleep, our bodies release a lot of hormones. These help control appetite, let our brain know when it's had enough food, and control food cravings. They also help us process sugar and use energy.

## Did You Know?

People naturally have a 24-hour cycle for waking and sleeping. This remains true even when outside light is cut off, such as when someone lives in a cave for months. Or the reverse, when people have nearly 24 hours of light, they still sleep!

## Sleep better

Many things can affect your sleep. You are a unique individual. What you need might not be the same as what someone else needs. But try these things to see if they help you sleep well. Good sleep practices are sometimes called sleep hygiene.

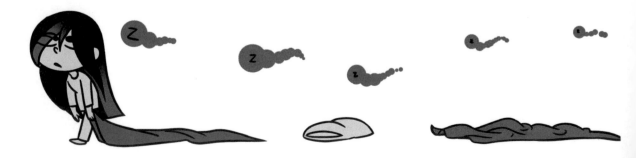

It's best to go to bed at the same time every night. This lets your body know it should expect to sleep at that time. If you have a dog in your house that likes to sleep with you, then you might notice that at about the same time each night your dog will start whining to go to sleep with you. Pets have good sense. Get up near the same time every day as well, even on the weekend. Staying up late and sleeping in on the weekend can make it harder to get back to your routine on Monday. No need to make those Mondays any harder.

A regular bedtime routine can tell your mind that it's time to sleep. For the hour before bed, do relaxing things like reading or writing in a journal or the relaxation exercises in Chapter 6. A warm bath can be relaxing, but don't make it too hot - it's harder to fall asleep if your body temperature is high.

If you lie in bed worrying, clearing your mind might help you sleep. Try writing down your problems in a notebook. Practice some relaxation techniques or try to think about things that make you happy.

If you do homework late in the evening, you might feel anxious or stressed about it. Try to finish your homework earlier so you have time to relax before bed.

Napping can be a good way to recharge during the day. But a nap does not make up for a bad night's sleep. Also, sleeping during the day can make it harder to fall asleep or stay asleep at night. If you need a nap, take a short one, only 10 to 20 minutes, and before 5 p.m. That way you have time to get tired again before bedtime.

## Food and drink

Some foods and drinks can interfere with sleep like caffeine. Caffeine is a stimulant, which means it makes you more alert. Caffeine is found in cola, tea and some other soft drinks. It's best to avoid eating food or drinking drinks with caffeine six hours before bedtime. This is especially important if you have ADHD.

Food can also affect your sleep. Eating a big meal close to bedtime might make it hard to sleep. Try to eat dinner several hours before bedtime. If you need a snack later, have something small that won't keep you awake.

Sleeping on your back is good because it doesn't twist your spine or put pressure on your neck. However, it can make snoring worse.

The best position for most people is sleeping on your side, with your knees bent. This puts the spine in a good position with no stress. You can put a pillow between your knees and hug it for even more comfort.

Sleeping with a pet nearby can be nice, but if the pet wakes up at night it might keep you from sleeping well. If your pet wakes you up a lot, try to keep it out of your room. Our dog, Obi-wan Kenobi, definitely won't let us sleep!

## Light

Light tells your brain to wake up. To make sure your room is dark enough at night, use heavy curtains over any windows. Or get blackout shades that are designed to keep out the light.

**Amazing Animals!**

- Some animals hibernate during the winter. This lets them survive months of cold darkness without having to search food. Hibernating animals aren't merely sleeping. Their temperature drops and their breathing slows so they can use less energy. They may lose a lot weight - up to half their body weight.

- Animals in the desert may go into a similar slow period during the summer to escape the heat. This is called aestivation. Earthworms, snails, and many amphibians and reptiles, including Nile crocodiles aestivate. Usually they bury themselves in the ground where the cool earth or mud protects them from the heat. Hibernation and aestivation may last a few months or even several years. A bacteria discovered on the Arctic seafloor 'woke up' after 100 million years! Other animals such as frogs and snails may wait years for conditions to be perfect before they wake up.

- Animals that sleep mostly at night and are active during the day like humans are called diurnal. Animals that sleep during the day and are active at night, such as bats or even many cat species, called are nocturnal.

And, of course, remember to turn off your lamp (in case that wasn't obvious enough).

You also need to make sure you don't have light coming from inside the room! Many electronic devices have small lights that shine all the time. These can add up to create a lot of light in the room. Turn off computers, stereos, and other devices at night.

Speaking of devices, don't use a phone or e-reader in bed. There are two reasons for this. Your bed should be used only for sleeping. You want your mind to associate being in bed with sleeping.

There's another reason electronic devices can be bad at bedtime. Many of them emit blue light. This kind of light confuses your body into thinking it's time to wake up. Some devices have an option for turning off blue light. Otherwise, avoid looking at a bright screen for 2 to 3 hours before bedtime.

An alarm clock might also have a light bright enough to disturb your sleep. Turn the brightness down or put some tape over it to dim the light. Also, if you keep looking at the clock, you might feel more stressed about not being able to sleep. Turn the clock away from you so you can't see the time on it from bed.

If you can't make your room dark enough, try using a sleeping mask. These masks cover your eyes to block the light. If you need a night light, get one that is as faint as possible. A dim red light is the best. Red light doesn't disturb sleep the way blue light does. Plus, red is really cool!

## Sunshine and exercise

Darkness is best when you want to sleep, but light is good when you want to wake up. Pull back your curtains when you get up.

Try to get outside in natural light for a few minutes every morning. Morning exercise can also help you feel awake. When you exercise, your body releases a hormone that makes you more alert. But exercise is also good for sleep. Gentle exercise, such as an evening walk or yoga can be relaxing.

## Did You Know?

Some people work at night and sleep during the day. This is called working the "night shift"( or being a vampire).

## Noise

It can be hard to sleep when your surroundings are noisy. A quiet room is best for most people, but silence is not always possible. "White noise" can help block out other sounds. White noise is a steady noise, like the sound of a fan.

## What to do

Take a look around your bedroom. Is it a calm, restful place that makes it easy to sleep? If not, what can you do to make it better? Start by making a list of problems to address. Then make a plan for how to fix those things. Finally, follow your plan!

Next, keep a sleep diary. The most important thing to know about getting a good night's sleep is this: every person is different. What works for your parents or siblings or friends might not work for you. Some people love white noise, while other people hate it. Some people can't eat before bed, while others need a small snack. To find out what you need, experiment! Remember, experiments are fun!

A sleep diary will help you figure out what works for you. It can also help you identify any serious sleep problems. If you suspect you have a sleep disorder such as sleep apnea or restless leg syndrom, see a doctor. Bring your sleep diary so you can share what you've learned.

Note: you're supposed to write in the diary when you're awake!

As you make changes, note how well you sleep! Every few weeks, look back over your diary to see if you can learn anything.

### Chapter 5: True or False Answers

1. We need sleep, just like we need food and water.

   True. Humans and other animals can't survive without sleep.

2. We spend one quarter of our lives asleep.

   False. We spend about a third of our lives sleeping. Do the math: 8 out of 24 hours.

3. You dream the entire time you're asleep.

   False. There are several stages of sleep. You may dream during different stages, but most dreaming happens during REM sleep.

4. Scientists don't really know why we sleep.

   True. Scientists have been exploring sleep for many years. They look at how humans and other animals sleep. They study what happens when someone does not get enough sleep. They have learned a lot, yet it's still hard to say exactly why we sleep. There may be several reasons. But scientists are always learning more! Of course, sometimes they find out, "Oops, we were wrong!". Science is never afraid to say "Oops".

5. Staying up late to study will make you smarter the next day.

   False. Spending more time studying may help you learn more. However, being tired makes it hard to remember things or pay attention in class. You're better off studying earlier in the day and getting a good night's sleep.

# Chapter 6
# Relax!

**True or False**

1. Meditation is a religious practice.

2. When you meditate, your mind should be completely empty.

3. You need a large block of time for meditation.

4. You can practice mindfulness as you do other things.

5. Meditating can make you a better student.

6. When you meditate, you can float off the ground. Okay, okay, we're sorry! Focus is important!

Find the answers at the end of the chapter.

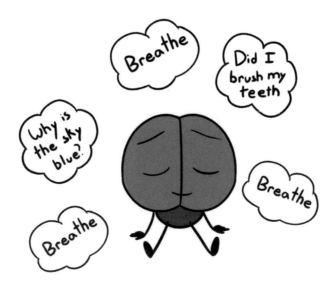

## What is meditation?

We all have a voice in our head. Often, this voice seems to focus on the negative. It tells you what you're doing wrong. It worries about what's going to happen next. It distracts you from what you're supposed to be doing now.

Meditating can help quiet the voice in your mind. It can help you focus and feel calm. It can even help you make decisions and be more disciplined. People who practice meditation can focus, concentrate, and do better in life. It can even make you less anxious and sad or depressed. It also helps people tolerate pain. It can often work better than medicines for calmness. Your mind can be a powerful thing!

The practice of meditation has been around for thousands of years. Today, science shows why it's so powerful. One study looked at people who were trained to meditate. After a few weeks, their brains showed improvements even when they weren't meditating!

## Did You Know?

Some religions practice meditation. However, meditation does not need to be religious. It has been shown by science to be helpful. Everyone can benefit from it regardless of your religious beliefs.

## Tip!

If you can't concentrate for very long, don't worry. It takes practice! You can find classes, online videos, and recordings that may help you learn to meditate.

## How to meditate

1. Sit in a comfortable place with your eyes closed. Any comfortable position is okay, as long as you won't fall asleep.

2. Breathe deeply. Take a long, slow breath in through your nose. Then let it out through your mouth. Focus on the breath only. Repeat. Feel your breath going in and out.

3. When your mind starts to wander, you'll think about all kinds of things: Why is the sky blue? Did I brush my teeth? Just go back to your breathing.

## How much is enough?

To start, try to meditate for 2-3 minutes once a day. After a few weeks, try to meditate twice a day. Then you can increase the time to five minutes for each session.

You can meditate more often if you like. Meditation in the morning may get the day off to a good start. Meditate before starting homework to focus your mind. Spending a few minutes focusing on your breathing may help you perform better in sports, music, or other activities. You can meditate as part of getting ready for bed, so you feel more relaxed. You can meditate whenever you feel anxious or stressed. It's nice if you can find a quiet place, but really, meditation works anywhere. You just need a quiet spot in your mind.

## Did You Know?

Some famous athletes practice meditation regularly. Entire professional sports teams sometimes learn and practice meditation together. Successful business people have also said meditation helps them in their work and daily lives. Some companies are making meditation part of the work schedule for all employees.

## Being mindful

"Mindfulness" is part of meditation. Being mindful means paying attention to what is happening now. Being aware now might sound easy, but it's hard for most of us, because our brain wants to zip off to other places. We stress about the past and future. Sometimes we entirely 'zone out' and forget about the world around us!

When you are mindful, you are focused on now. You are not worried about what happened 2 minutes ago or the test in 2 days. You are focused on the present. Think about it, if you can't change the past or the future, there's no need to worry about it! Thinking like this can help you quiet that evil voice in your head and replace it with the superhero voice that tells you, you can do anything!'

### Tip!

It's hard to be mindful when you're on a cell phone, computer, or other devices. Put down the electronics and focus on the real world when you need to be focusing on the real world. Though there are meditation apps!

Okay, class, now breathe in and... ouuuut...

**Tip!**

A great time to practice mindfulness is when you're eating. How does the food look? How does it smell? Taste? Don't watch T.V., play on a device, or read at the same time.

You become mindful by paying attention to the world around you. Tune into your senses. What do you see? What do you hear? Smell? Feel? Calmly focus on those feelings.

This can help you enjoy your food more and help you control what and how much you eat. When other thoughts enter your mind, accept them. They may or may not be true. They may or may not be important later. It doesn't matter right now. Acknowledge them and imagine those thoughts floating past you. Then go back to your senses and your breathing.

Of course, if there's something you should be doing now, do it. Mindfulness doesn't mean ignoring your homework or your chores. Instead, it means keeping your focus on what you're doing. You can practice mindfulness as part of meditation, or whenever you have a quiet moment. You can also try to be mindful when you're studying, exercising, or doing other activities. If you find yourself doing one thing and thinking about other things, try to let go of those thoughts. Focus on what you're doing now.

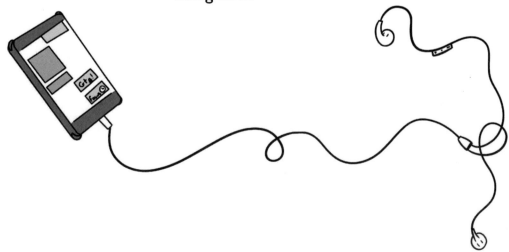

## Focus on your body

Some forms of meditation and mindfulness ask you to examine your body. You can start at your head and work down to your feet.

Or you can start with your feet and work up to your head. How does that part feel? Is it tense or in pain? Try tightening the muscles and then relaxing them. When you get to your torso, note your breathing. How does your belly move with your breath? How does your chest move?

This is a good time to think about your posture as well.

Not this one, though!

How does it feel when you straighten your back. If you notice tension in your shoulders, try relaxing them. Make sure your neck is long and straight, not scrunched up. Think like a giraffe!

Eureka! I just discovered Relativity!

While you're examining your body, you may have other thoughts. Note them and let them go, then let the thoughts float away instead of dwelling on them for now.

Note: this does not mean your homework will disappear!

## More meditation techniques

Try starting your meditation by picturing a peaceful place. It could be a beach, a forest, or the top of a mountain. Pick someplace calming to you. Picture it all around you. See the details. It may sound strange, but picturing a different place can help you focus on the real world when you come back from your imaginary journey. Think of it as getting lost in a movie in your mind.

Gazing Meditation uses an object to help you focus. You can try lighting a candle and placing it a few feet away (you should get an adult's permission and help for that!). Focus on the flame for a minute or two, then close your eyes and imagine the flame. When other thoughts enter your mind, imagine sending them into the fire.

You can also use a sound when you meditate. Some people use the sound 'Om' while meditating, and it's probably the first thing you think of when someone says 'meditation'. Or try a mantra. A mantra is a sound, word, or phrase that expresses your goals or beliefs. For example, you might choose "calm" if you want to be calm. It can be a statement like "I am strong", "I am focused", "I'm so full! Shouldn't have eaten that much!". Well, maybe not the last one. It can be spiritual or religious. Repeat the mantra over and over as you meditate. You can say it out loud, only in your mind, or both. Whatever works!

### Did You Know?

You know how you can visualize something in your head? Some people can't do this because of a weird disease called aphantasia. Almost 1 in 50 people have this! That's a lot! If you think you have this, don't worry. Your brain is special, not messed up! And it won't affect your memory because there are other memory techniques that don't require visualization

## Feeling grateful

Gratitude causes changes in your brain activity. These changes help you feel better and calmer. In fact, feeling grateful acts in the same way as some drugs that people take to fight depression. Even trying to feel grateful helps. So if you find yourself worrying a lot, practice gratitude. Even when times are hard, you can be grateful for your amazing brain, your awesome body, or even just your favorite smoothie!

For extra power, express your gratitude. Tell someone you're glad to have them in your life. Tell your friends and family about the little things you enjoy each day. Keep a diary and list something you're grateful for each day. Get in the habit of noticing good things, big or small. Your words and thoughts have the power to make you and others feel better.

## Label your emotions

Naming your emotions can help you handle those emotions. Simply putting a label on an emotion changes your brain activity. If you feel sad, anxious, or angry, name the emotion. Recognizing how you feel can help you feel better. On the other hand, trying to ignore your feelings doesn't work.

Your brain keeps feeling those emotions even if you try to hide them. You can tell someone else how you feel, write it down, or simply spend a few minutes thinking about it. After you acknowledge the emotion, it's easier to let it go.

You can label your thoughts as well. Maybe the voice in your head keeps telling you you're going to fail at something. Give that speech a name. Then when those thoughts invade your mind, tell yourself, "Oh, that's the 'mess up' speech. I don't need that right now."

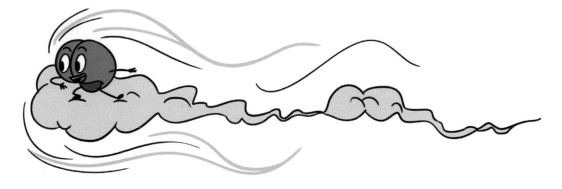

## Make a decision

It can be hard to make decisions when you feel anxious or overwhelmed. Yet making a decision can help you feel calmer. Making a decision affects your brain in ways that reduce anxiety and worry.

Of course, sometimes making a decision is hard. Start by making some small decisions. "I'm going to do my English homework first." "I'm going to eat an apple as a snack." "I'm going to wear my underwear on the outside of my clothes!". Also, if you can't think of a great decision, choose the one that's best of all the options. They don't have to be absolutely perfect!

What if later, the decision seems wrong? Remind yourself that you made the best decision you could at the time. No one can predict the future. No one knows for sure how other people will react. Things can and will change. You can learn from what went wrong. Then, you can make a better decision next time!

The important thing to take away is that things happen that you can't predict or control. That's not your fault. Accept what happened, try to let it go, and move on.

## Did You Know?

Making a decision gives your brain a pleasure boost! That doesn't happen if someone makes the decision for you, though you can certainly accept their feedback. If you want to do well in school only because someone else wants you to, it's harder. If you try to exercise or eat healthy because you think you're supposed to, it's harder. You don't get that pleasure boost unless you decide it's what you should do. That's why it's so important to decide what you want, now and for the future. If you choose, you'll find it easier to reach your goals.

### Chapter 6: True or False Answers

I. Meditation is a religious practice.

Partly true. Some Religions include meditation. However, many people use meditation separately from religion.

2. When you meditate, your mind should be completely empty.

False. An empty mind can be a goal, but it may not happen. The important thing is to focus on the moment and let go of other thoughys. Plus, when you think about it, a completely empty mind probably isn't a good thing.

3. You need a large block of time for meditation.

False. Meditating for even a few minutes can help focus and calm your mind.

4. You can practice mindfulness as you do other things.

True! You can practice mindfulness during meditation. You can also try it while eating, exercising, or doin other activities.

5. Meditating can make you a better student.

True. Learning to meditate can help with focus, which is important for learning and memory.

# Chapter 7
# Planning: Get Smart!

**True or False**

1. Setting goals is only one step in reaching goals.

2. Goals should focus on school success.

3. You should set goals that will be easy to reach.

4. If you fail to reach a goal, there's nothing more you can do.

5. You should tell other people your goals.

6. If your goal is to be a hockey goalie, then you have a goalie goal! Ha, just making sure you're still reading!

Find the answers at the end of the chapter.

We've shared a lot of information in the earlier chapters. We hope we got you excited about making changes. We hope you have thoughts on how you can live a healthier, smarter life. But wanting to change doesn't do much good by itself. You need a plan for how to make that change happen. You can sit on the couch wishing you were a better athlete, or you can start exercising and practicing your skills. Which option do you think will work? Hint: It's not the first one. You might want better grades but you spend your time playing video games, or you could be practicing memory tricks, study harder, or get any tutoring help you need. What's likely to happen with each choice? Hint: the first one isn't going to improve your grades unless you're taking a video game class!.

You can sit at home alone hoping for more friends, or you can join activities where you'll meet people. Which path has the best chance of success for what you want? Hint: It might be easier to connect with people online if you have social anxiety, but you still have to try to make friends if you want some! Make sure it's alright with your parents first.

SMART is an acronym. That means it's an abbreviation for several words, which is one of the memory tricks. The first letter of each word makes the acronym. In this case, the words are:

## Specific
## Measurable
## Achievable
## Relevant (to your bigger goals)
## Time bound (have them done within a certain time)

Your goals works if it fits these measures.
The acronym SMART can help you remember them. (SMART can help you be smart!)

**SPECIFIC**

**MEASURABLE**

**ACHIEVABLE**

**RELEVANT** (to your bigger goals)

**TIMEBOUND** (done within a certain time)

Your goal works if it fits these measures.

The acronym **SMART** can help you remember them. **SMART** can help you be smart!

Let's start by setting some goals. First, think big. Where do you want to be in one year? Five years? When you grow up? Maybe you want to play on a high school sports team. Maybe you'd like to be a famous musician, dancer, or other kind of artist, a scientist, astronaut, teacher, doctor, or journalist. Go ahead and write those goals down. If you don't know what you want to be when you grow up, that's fine. You have lots of time to figure it out, and you can always change your mind. But if you do know what you want from your future, write them down!

Okay, now let's back up a bit (make a beeping noise if you'd like! Beep, beep, beep - okay, that's far enough). Save those ideas you wrote down and address how you plan to get there as you get through this chapter of the book. Planning can sometimes be overwhelming. Lets take it slow and plan the SMART way!

## Be SMART everywhere

SMART goals can be used for all areas of life - physical health, mental health, academic achievement and more.

You can plan for a career, explore music, practice spirituality, build leadership skills, and find ways to help or serve others. Setting goals and tracking them weekly or even daily can help you reach success with any and all of these things. Plus, tracking things is fun!

## Think about these areas of your life:

- Academics: A goal might be to get or maintain all B's in your classes, or to improve your grade in one class. You could also set goals around improving your study habits. Health: Goals could involve making specific changes in your diet, like maybe you want to eat less sugar, try a plant-based diet, or just eat more vegetables than you currently do. Goals could also address specific health challenges you face.

- Sports and hobbies: Maybe you want to learn a new skill, make a sports team, or try out for the next school play. Or you could set aside time each week for art, music, or other creative activities. Call it your 'me time'. Everyone needs some me time. You might want to make new friends, or get closer to your current friends. You might want to spend more time with your family! Other goals could be about learning to communicate better or practicing good listening.

**Tip!**

It may feel like you don't have enough time for the things you want to do. Are there activities that are wasting your time?

- Relaxation/Stress: If you feel stressed and busy all the time, a good goal might be to spend half an hour every day relaxing. You could try meditation techniques or yoga. If you have problems with anger, you might want to learn how to manage your emotions. Getting a good night's sleep could also fit into this category!

- Home skills: You might want to earn or save money every week. You could learn to cook, repair torn clothes, or take up gardening. You could also shovel or rake leaves for neighbors in the winter or fall. You can make money and get a workout that way!

- Organization: Is your room cluttered? We'll guess yes! A goal might be to clean it weekly so you can find things more easily. Do you have trouble with time management? Set goals that will help you learn better time management skills. Are you easily distracted? Take some time to learn techniques to minimize distractions.

- Environment: Is nature important to you? Do you care about animals? You could set goals around being a good citizen of the Earth. Maybe you want to help your family or school recycle more. You could learn ways to pollute less, or volunteer at an animal shelter.

- Charity: Are there causes that are important to you? Do you want to donate your time to help with a charity? How about raising money?

If you're not sure where your time is going, keep a diary for a week or so. Write down what you do every hour.

You may be surprised at how much time you put into certain things. Note: if you're spending a significant amount of time in the bathroom, talk to your doctor. Many people spend a lot of time watching T.V., being on social media, or playing on the computer. We're not saying you shouldn't ever watch T.V. or play a game. After all, everybody needs a little fun now and then. But you have to ask yourself, "Do these things bring me closer to my goals?". If not, you should limit how much time you spend on them.

## Be SMART

Now you may have some goals, or at least some ideas about goals. It's time to get SMART.

So let's start with the "S" in SMART. It stands for Specific, and a specific goal is clear and detailed. Goals such as, "I want to do better in school" or "I want to be more popular" are too non-specific! How are you going to achieve them? Think about what you want to accomplish and why it's important to you. How clear and specific can you be? A specific goal is "I want to do well in Math Class", with math being the specific element.

The "M" in SMART stands for Measurable. A measurable goal is one you can track. It might involve a deadline for success. It might have numbers associated with 'how much' or 'how many'. In super-duper fancy terms, it's quantifiable. Use that word on your parents, they'll be impressed! Numbers can help you feel motivated and in control. They can also help you keep on track. You know exactly what you have to do to succeed.

"I will do well in school" is not a measurable goal. "I will bring my English grade up to an A" is more measurable. "I will score 95 out of 100 on my next math test is measurable. When you get your grades, you will know you've succeeded. "I will eat healthier" is not measurable. "I will drink no more than three cans of soda every week" is.

"I will be more social" isn't either. "I will make three new friends this year" targets a specific number. The "A" in SMART goals is Achievable. An achievable goal is a realistic one. It's something you're likely able to achieve. That doesn't mean it'll be easy, but it should be possible. If you never run, becoming the star of your track team this season is not realistic.

Winging an Olympic gold medal in the next Olympics would be even less realistic, at least for a short-term goal. Oh, that reminds us: if you have long-term goals, be sure to break them into short-term goals. But back on the subject of achievable goals - a realistic goal might be to simply join the team and learn to run. You can dream big from there!

The "R" in SMART goals stands for Relevant. A Relevant goal serves your bigger purpose.

Will it help you become the person you want to be? Does it work with your other goals? Does it work with your family and friends? Is this the right time for that goal? This one might require some hard thinking. So this is how this one works: it makes you think about the bigger goals you have in life, and then see if the SMART goals you're making are going to help you achieve those big life goals. For example, if a big life goal is to become an engineer, is getting an "A" in your math class going to help?

## Tip!

Your goals may change over time. You may also need to change short-term goals in order to reach your long-term goals. It's a good idea to check on your goals on a regular basis. You might check them on the first day of every month. Or you could review your weekly goals on Sunday nights. Set a reminder so you don't forget! If you want to make your phone feel useful you can set reminders with it!

Finally, the "T" in SMART stands for Timebound. A timebound goal has a deadline. You already know you need a way to measure success. When will it happen? By the end of the semester? The year? Next year? Remember that people are not very good at estimating the time it will take to achieve something. We tend to remember our successes without taking into account all the setbacks we faced, so give yourself time.

Of course, some goals may be lifelong ones! If you want to eat a healthier diet, you can't say "I did it, I'm done!" Instead, the deadline might be to start the goal. "In the next two months, I will try ten new fruits and vegetables. Then, I'll decide what I like and make sure I get five servings of fresh produce every day". You can still check on your goals, too. Every week or month, ask yourself if you're still achieving that goal.

Are these still the goals you want to reach? Do you need to change your goals, or change your plans to reach them?

If you haven't succeeded yet, don't get discouraged. You don't have to give up the goal. You might need to change it to make it more realistic for you, or your might just need a new plan.

If you tried your best, give yourself credit for trying. If you didn't try very hard, why not? Maybe that's not the best goal for you, after all. Or maybe you need a new plan. Keep trying!

**Hint!**

Whenever you succeed in accomplishing a goal or a step towards a goal, give yourself a little reward. A little positive reinforcement helps you use and repeat positive actions. Think of it as training your brain!

## Write it down

It's important to write down your goals. It's also important to put them somewhere you can see them regularly. There's a saying, "Out of sight, out of mind". It means that if you don't see something, you tend to forget about it. So put your goals on a poster on the wall, or on the calendar, or in a notebook you use every day!

You also need to write down weekly and daily goals. This might work best on a calendar. You can schedule time slots for when you want to work on each thing that day.

You can also spend a few minutes every morning thinking about your goals for the day. Ask yourself, "What three things do I want to accomplish by tonight?" Don't make them too easy like "eat breakfast, say hi to bobby, eat lunch". Goals should be a little challenging!

**Tip!**

Pictures can also remind you of your goals and help motivate you.

Make a vision board! For each of your goals, draw pictures, or cut pictures out of magazines. Do you want to learn how to cook? Find some pictures of tasty dishes you'd like to try. You might also find recipes to try too!

Friendly Reminder: If you've never turned the stove on before, you may want to ask your parents for help.

## Share your goals

Another way to stay motivated is to tell people about your goals. Share with people who will encourage you to succeed. Even better, share with people who have similar goals. You can encourage each other that way. You can check in often and see where you are. Maybe you can work together. For example, say you have a goal to take a 30 minute walk 3 times a week. Find a buddy to walk with!

Some people might discourage you from trying to reach your goals. They might call your goals silly or stupid. Don't share your goals or interests with those people.

Sometimes, other people can see things more clearly than we can. Especially, if those people are the ones who really care about us. Make sure you talk to people you know and trust to support and trust you. If you say, "I want to climb Mount Everest!" and a bunch of people you love and trust say, "Yeah but aren't you afraid of heights? Maybe try something else, or work up to Everest!" In that case, you might want to think about their words - listen to people you trust!

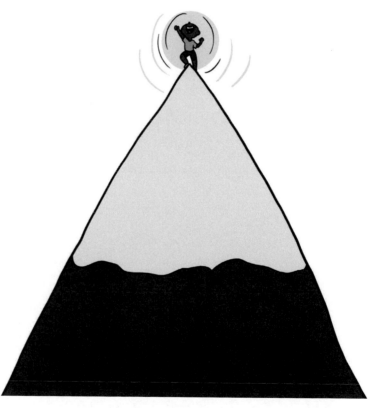

## Chapter 7: True or False Answers

1. Setting goals is only one step in reaching goals.

   True. After setting goals, you should develop a plan for how you're going to reach those goals.

2. Goals should focus on school success.

   False. You can set goals for every part of your life: diet, exercise, sleep, relaxation, and much more. Of course, you can have school goals, too!

3. You should set goals that will be easy to reach.

   False. It should be possible to reach your goals. They should be reasonably achievable. That does not mean they need to be easy. If you really want something, work hard to achieve it!

4. If you fail to reach a goal, there's nothing more you can do.

   False. If you don't reach your goal, try to figure out what happened. Maybe you need a new plan. Maybe you need more time than you originally thought. Make a new plan and keep going.

5. You should tell other people your goals.

   True. Sharing your goals can help you feel motivated. It's even better if you can work together with a friend or family member. Just make sure you find people who will encourage and support you!

# In Conclusion

You are unique. You have unique strengths, talents, and qualities to give to the world. You can find meaning, joy, and great fun in your uniqueness. In other words, accept who you are! Like yourself for being yourself; there's a lot to like. There is no right or wrong way to live a life.

You aren't perfect, but no one is. Perfection is pretty much an impossible dream, and it's impossible to define.

Work to better yourself, but don't sweat it if 'better' doesn't come easily or quickly. There's nothing wrong with having weak areas. Everybody has weak areas. Superman has kryptonite, Batman can be stubborn. Nobody is perfect, not even your mom. The key is to accept that you have those weak areas. Know that you have them and work on ways of making yourself better at them. Sometimes, just accepting weakness is a huge start.

Nobody is an island. Remember you have friends and family to help you! We're all part of a big team called the human race, and while humans might be a race, we're not really in a competition with each other. In fact, the more we work together and cooperate, the more we can all get done. All of this starts with knowing and accepting yourself. Only then can you make positive changes. You'll have good interactions with others. People who know and like themselves can become leaders and helpers in this world. If you like yourself, others will like you too. The key is to be happy! Your brain is a powerful tool that you can mend or mold however you wish. Your mood is set by your thoughts. Use positive reinforcement on yourself and those around you. If you do something that makes you happy or makes you feel better, give yourself a little reward. Remember to tell and thank others when they do positive things for you.

We believe if you incorporate all these habits into your life, you will be able to bring out the full force of that amazing brain of yours. The key to becoming SUPER YOU is to start with a couple of habits that you believe are achievable and build on these habits with each success. Follow the book to find your own way to be a SUPER YOU, and remember that we believe in you!

## Alex Sherzai

Alex was doing Calculus at age 8, finished high school at age 10, took the SAT at 10 and was the first person to ever score in the 90th percentile at that age. He was also the youngest person to have his research abstract accepted at a national conference. He co-wrote his first book (Walk Like An Elephant) at age 10 with his sister, Sophia, and spoke at March for Science Los Angeles in 2017 and 2018. Alex is also a pianist and music composer.

## Sophia Sherzai

Sophia was reading fluently at age 2, finished high school at 10, took the Pre-SAT at 10 and scored in the 90th percentile. She is an amazing singer and loves music. Along with her brother Alex, she co-wrote their first book, spoke at March For Science, and manages their nonprofit organization, The Science Kids Foundation, which is dedicated to supporting Science and Health in communities.

Made in the USA
San Bernardino, CA
12 June 2020